Lex Naturalis

A Journal of Natural Law Volume 4 Fall 2019

Pace University Press
41 Park Row, 15th Floor
New York, NY 10038

ISBN: 978-1-935625-36-0
ISSN: 2474-8994

Lex Naturalis

CONTENTS

VOLUME 4 **FALL 2019**

BOOK REVIEWS

Editor's Note:

Beginning with this issue, together with new essays and book reviews, *Lex Naturalis* will include summaries of the topics discussed at each year's American Maritain Association conference, courtesy of Greg Kerr. Jacques Maritain, of course, was one of the leading neo-Thomists of the twentieth century, and his commentaries on Aquinas's texts on natural law have been central to recent and contemporary discussions of the topic.

— W.R.

Hans Jonas's Ontological Ethics and the Natural Law

Julia Bolzon

The concern of twentieth-century German Jewish philosopher Hans Jonas was to develop a philosophy of the living being that re-thought the problem of Cartesian dualism and its "divorce of the material and mental."[1] His insistence on a non-dualistic ontology, one that recovered a more adequate philosophy of nature, dovetailed with his desire to counter nihilism, which he claimed to be at the heart of Martin Heidegger's philosophy of being. Moreover, Jonas's awareness that nihilism actually posed a *danger* to mankind was solidified in the face of the unprecedented powers of modern technology, specifically atomic warfare and genetic engineering. The apocalyptic potential of technology, writes Jonas, "raises the metaphysical question never posed to ethics before: whether and why there ought to be a mankind?"[2] Thus, his work aims at showing why the future of mankind ought to be preserved, and more pointedly, why this burden of responsibility addressed to man is an *ontological* imperative, inherent in being itself.

The ontological character of Jonas's theory of responsibility is what enables one to draw a comparison between his ethics and the natural law, insofar as both seek to affirm the presence of an axiological element in nature itself. A further grounds for comparison is the role of God or theology, for Jonas's theory seems to bear similarities, *mutatis mutandis,* to the new natural law theory of John Finnis, which self-professedly does not depend upon God or the Eternal Law for its intelligibility.[3] Indeed, Lawrence Vogel describes Jonas's ethics as a "minimalist version" of natural law because of its ontological rather than theological grounding, showing that while a theology of creation can supplement Jonas's theory, it need not.[4] Unlike Vogel, for whom the non-necessity of theology to Jonas's ethics lends it its natural-law character, I argue the opposite: it is precisely because his thought is buoyed from within by his Jewish roots, and therefore bears an implicit theology, that it maintains a great affinity with the biblical-Thomistic natural law tradition. While not a "version" of natural law itself, Jonas's work harbours fruitful points of contact with this tradition that are apt for studying, not only because he offers a philosophical attempt to retrieve an adequate notion of nature, but also because he seeks to articulate an ethics that is not ultimately reducible to relativism or positivism. This article will present a brief overview of Jonas's ontological ethics and look more closely at the role theology plays in his thought, before identifying the areas of resonance between his thought and the natural law that need to be developed and deepened.

Re-Thinking the Foundation of Being

Hans Jonas tells us the following in his *Memoirs*:

> It's my conviction…that ontology necessarily entails a doctrine of obligation. But is that really true? Can an objective perception of being, one whose premises don't point it in a specific direction, but which represents an objective, neutral ontology, yield a doctrine of values or even a doctrine of duties?…I felt I had to take the risk of suggesting that values were more than a matter of subjective choice, the risk of deriving certain obligations from being, for I'm sure that I'm right about this, even if I haven't succeeded in completely working out the proof that being can tell us something about how we should live, but above all about the responsibilities that we human beings, acting consciously and freely, must fulfill.[5]

In this passage, Jonas connects the dots between his "philosophy of the organic" and his "ethics of responsibility," which he first began thinking about during the Second World War while serving with the Jewish brigade of the British army.[6] As a philosopher immersed in the chaos of war, Jonas was inspired to re-think the very foundations of being. His first dominant concern was the fact that the reigning philosophy of German idealism—whether neo-Kantian, phenomenological, or existential—had an exclusive focus on the mind to the detriment of the "organic basis" by which the mind exists at all, namely, the body. Jonas perceived that this holdover from Cartesian dualism effectively "prejudged the ontological question from its roots," and thus he identified dualism as needing to be rethought from the locus of the organism.[7]

Jonas sought to remedy the exclusively anthropocentric focus of contemporary existentialism to better understand the "dimension of *inwardness*" that belongs to all of organic life.[8] By "inwardness" Jonas means the presence of a subjective or "inner" dimension common to living being; he sees no definitive break, no "line" demarcating a "before" and "after" in terms of the presence of both mind and freedom in animate being.[9] There is a psycho-physical unity to life that, while still upholding a distinction between mind and matter, nevertheless sees mind pre-figured in non-rational substances. This is what leads Jonas to describe the dimension of inwardness as "coextensive with life" as such.[10] His first book, *The Phenomenon of Life: Toward a Philosophical Biology*, sought to recover our awareness of the existence of this "inner dimension" to life and to show what it means for ethics: the very interiority of nature is the ground for an ethics of responsibility. Jonas interprets the emergence of mind from seemingly "mindless material" existentially, as indicative of a non-indifferent nature. In other words, nature/living being is not "indifferent" in the sense of being neutral, "empty" or value-void. Rather, living being bears a basic value by virtue of its striving for life in the face of death; moreover, only the human being is able to recognize and take responsibility for this obligation which nature inherently poses, if properly attuned to it.[11] In this way, Jonas sees a principle of ethics, namely, obligation, ultimately grounded in "an objective assignment by the nature of things."[12]

Jonas on the Task of Ethics

Jonas is known for wanting to establish a "new" ethics for our age. He sees the technological ability of modern man, and its unprecedented consequences, as having rendered traditional ethics ill-equipped and ultimately incapable of offering norms to guide man's action.[13] There are two prongs to Jonas's ontological ethics: responsibility *for* and responsibility *to.* The former refers to man needing to be accountable for his technological abilities; man as the source or origin—the "great creator of the danger"—of modern technology.[14] The latter refers to what we have outlined above in terms of the meaning of organic life, namely that there is an obligation written into being itself that says, "take care of me." It is this claim of our ontological responsibility to nature that needs greater explaining.

A key contention of Jonas is that a philosophy of life, which consists of a philosophy of both mind and organism, also contains an ethics.[15] This is why the duty toward future generations is not solely deontological, but primarily ontological: "Duty needs to be perceived in order to be followed, *but it exists even if not perceived* and *must therefore possess its own independent ground*."[16] Man's responsibility for his actions and his responsibility to nature (his obligation or duty to preserve humanity's existence) are flip sides of the same coin. While it is easier to recognize that man has a responsibility *for* (i.e. his actions), because he is a free, rational being, how is this also indicative of his responsibility *to* something, (i.e. an obligation)? Jonas says whenever we are confronted with a being of value (and here is the rub: there is no such thing as a value-indifferent being, for Jonas), we are met with a claim of responsibility to that being:

> If now (and whenever) there is the assumption—again an *ontological* one—that what exists is of value, then *its* being will have a claim on me; and since the valuableness of Being as a whole speaks to me via this special instance, then ultimately this whole does not appear solely as that *for* which I *become* responsible with my actions in this particular case but also as that *to* which I *have* always *been* responsible with all my possible actions—since its *value* has a *justified claim* on me.[17]

Jonas's prime illustration of this phenomenon is the parent-child relationship. In the non-reciprocal (or "one-sided") responsibility of parent to child, Jonas finds the archetype of responsibility as such. Specifically, we see this when faced with a newborn, "whose mere breathing uncontradictably addresses an ought to the world around, namely, to take care of him. Look and you know."[18] He specifies that the newborn's existence poses an obligation as opposed to a mere entreaty, and characterizes this as "the elemental 'ought' in the 'is' of the newborn."[19] By illustrating how our obligation (responsibility *to*) arises from the value of being, Jonas is showing that the ground of our obligation or responsibility is thus objective, i.e. rooted in being itself, and not something we merely enter into as if by contract. Jonas is well aware of the "is-ought" objection, which he directly engages with throughout *The Imperative of Responsibility.* He challenges the axiomatic claim of the non-derivability of an "ought" from an "is," which "is only true for a concept of being that has been suitably neutralized beforehand (as "value free")—so that the nonderivability of an 'ought' from it follows tautologically."[20] For Jonas, "Being, in the testimony it gives of itself, informs us not only about what it is but also about what we owe to it."[21]

The (Ambiguous) Role of Theology in Jonas's Ethics

Lawrence Vogel argues that Jonas presents a "natural law" theory of responsibility because his ethics does not depend on revelation, theology, or Scripture for its validity.[22] Vogel writes that "as a philosopher…Jonas insists that his imperative of responsibility can be 'ontologically' grounded without appealing to theistic premises, for 'an image of man' is rooted in 'the integrity of nature' even if nature is not God's creation."[23] Indeed, Vogel describes Jonas as "translating" theological propositions into naturalistic ones, with the claim that there is "no *need* to ground ontology in theology, for nature is purposive even if there is no 'purposer.'"[24] Elsewhere Vogel clarifies that although Jonas engages with theological concepts in the course of working out his ethics, his project does not inherently depend upon them: "It may seem…that theology provides the only alternative to the nihilism of modern reason, but I think that Jonas's metaphysics should be read as an attempt to preserve the meaning of…biblical propositions on rational grounds without relying on theology at all."[25]

Moreover, he tells us Jonas "explicitly denies that nature needs to be created by God in order to ground an imperative of responsibility."[26]

It is true that Jonas variously writes that ethics does not depend on theology. The reason, as he presents it, is the "eclipse of revelation," by which he seems to mean the untenability of the idea of a divine order and belief in God in the modern world.[27] This is the stance he had articulated early on in his thought, stating that "an ethics no longer founded on divine authority must be founded on a principle discoverable in the nature of things, lest it fall victim to subjectivism or other forms of relativity."[28] Jonas was concerned with showing that man does have an obligation, that ethics really is rooted in our being, regardless of whether or not man believes in a divine authority. Given the circumstances of secular modernity, an ethics rooted in *nature* is the only viable non-arbitrary basis for Jonas: "where norms for the use of the optional new powers are called for, an image of Man must provide their nonarbitrary basis; and with the eclipse of revelation, this image is the sole responsibility of philosophy."[29] According to Jonas, "a commandment can proceed from the being of things themselves—not initially from the will of a personal Creator God on their behalf—and can be intended for me," because obligation exists in *being* itself; the ought-to-be of being, which is a fact of its being in existence at all, implies an "ought-to-do of someone in response."[30] This ontological rooting of responsibility is what allows Jonas to say that responsibility exists "with or without God."[31]

Yet familiarity with Jonas's work suggests that the role of theology in his thought, and therefore his ethics, may be more than simply marginal.[32] Mentions of theological principles, such as the sovereignty of God, the world as created, and man as the *imago Dei* occur not only in his early writings but also throughout the entirety of his corpus.[33] With respect to ethics, Jonas is well aware of its original, theological foundation, what he identifies as the *ordo creationis*—the biblical notion of the world as God's good creation, and of man as made in His image:

> Ontology as the ground of ethics was the original tenet of philosophy. Their divorce, which is the divorce of the "objective" and "subjective" realms, is the modern destiny. Their reunion can be effected, if at all, only from the "objective" end, that is to say, through a revision of the idea of nature.... Hence would result a principle of ethics which is ultimately grounded neither in the autonomy of the self nor in the needs of the community, but in an objective assignment by the nature of things (what theology used to call the *ordo creationis*).[34]

He returns to religion as the ground for ethics in the speech he gave six days before his death:

> It was once religion which told us that we all are sinners, because of original sin. It is now the ecology of our planet which pronounces us all to be sinners because of the excessive exploits of human inventiveness. It was once religion which threatened us with a last judgment at the end of days. It is now our tortured planet which predicts the arrival of such a day without any heavenly intervention. The latest revelation—from no Mount Sinai, from no Mount of the Sermon, from no Bo (tree of Buddha)—is the outcry of mute things themselves that we must heed by curbing our powers over creation, lest we perish together on a wasteland of what was creation.[35]

While one can say, as Vogel does, that Jonas has a Jewish theology that merely supplements his ontological vision of nature, I argue that the theological retains a primacy in Jonas's thought, not as having a central role or explicit presence, but in the sense of an ontological priority. That is, if the biblical Judaeo-Christian concept of creation was operative in Jonas's thought from the beginning (and not added as an "appendage"), then it has an actual priority or primacy in his thought, even if it remains "in the background" or implicit.

Although Jonas explicitly insists that ethics is anchored in metaphysics and not theology, this does not mean that theological considerations are (at best) supplementary or (at worst) irrelevant to his thought.[36] The theological is not a supplement or appendage to Jonas's thought, but rather plays a tacitly vital role, as I hope to show. I think that Vogel's description of Jonas's "ontological analog" for theological ideas, i.e. the claim that he "translates" theological propositions into naturalistic ones, too quickly elides the two so that the implicit priority of the theological disappears. Natural law—although ontological, that is, discoverable by reason because it is "written" *in* the very being of things—is itself not devoid of theology, because it depends on eternal law for its very existence: God's providential ordering and governing of the cosmos. Jonas's ethics does not comprise natural law in the full sense, for it lacks a thoroughgoing theocentric character.[37] However, the profound openness within Jonas's thought to a robust sense of the natural law is due to the implicit animating role of theology.

Hans Jonas: "Philosopher and Jew"[38]

While Vogel says it is unclear whether Jonas's philosophy of nature is informed by his Judaism, or whether he is a philosopher "who happens to be Jewish," the work of Christian Wiese on the Jewish dimensions of Jonas's thought helps us to see the constant recurrence of the theological. Wiese argues that Hans Jonas is a "profoundly Jewish non-Jewish Jew," such that his being a philosopher *and* being a Jew inform one another from within.[39] Jonas did not want to be recognized as a "Jewish philosopher," Wiese explains, "not only because he feared…that such a label would situate his philosophy and the ethics he formulated for a global technological civilization in a particularistic Jewish canon, thus limiting its persuasive power as a universal philosophical approach," but also because "his philosophical ethos demanded that reason take unconditional precedence over any kind of personal religious ties."[40] Thus, it was both a matter of philosophical method—which Jonas describes as needing to be "atheistic"—and for the sake of the credibility of his ethical project that Jonas proceeded in "universal terms, without reference to religious or theological categories, lest it appeared as dogmatic or irrelevant," according to Wiese.[41]

Yet, while Jonas thinks "philosophy must proceed on the basis of disbelief," he was also of the view that "no 'secularization' may go so far that we forfeit the awareness or intuitions of transcendence which religion has made accessible and from which an inalienable content can be salvaged into the post-religious perspective."[42] The "inalienable content" in reference is that of the biblical *Imago Dei,* which Jonas rephrases in "symbolic shorthand" as the "image of Man."[43] More predominantly, the concept of creation is a recurring motif in Jonas's work. According to Wiese, it "is among the decisive aspects of his philosophical approach," which he describes as "the vanishing point at which the lines of [Jonas's] Jewish religious convictions and his philosophical arguments come into contact."[44] Jonas conveys the theological notion of creation through the idea of life's sacredness: "It is moot whether, without restoring the category of the *sacred,* the category most thoroughly destroyed by the scientific enlightenment, we can have an ethics able to cope with the extreme powers which we possess today."[45] Indeed, Jonas sought to help mankind retain a sense of humility and awe before the sacred in the world: "Caution is the urgent need for the hour. It will make us go slow on discarding old taboos, on brushing aside in our projects the sacrosanctity of certain domains hitherto surrounded by a sense of mystery, awe, and shame."[46]

Thus, while as a philosopher Jonas insists on the rational, ontological grounds for ethics, he never eschews the idea of creation outright, but instead operates in the framework that this reality is obscured from the modern mind. In other words, it does not seem that Jonas is declaring a complete severance of ethics from theology, but only an epistemological independence: one does not need to believe the truth of Revelation or theological principles to recognize humanity's obligation. Wiese writes, "Jonas hoped to establish a nonreligious foundation for the 'sanctity of life' that the secular world would accept," on the premise that religion is eclipsed for the modern man.[47] He argues that in spite of Jonas's attempts to "secularize" his own thought, the theological was present from the very beginning in the form of Jewish elements, namely, that of the createdness of all life, and that this is what Jonas wished to incorporate into Western philosophy.[48] In Wiese's estimation:

> Jonas deemphasized this theological component in the course of presenting his model of an autonomous ethics for the future in order not to endanger its universal plausibility.…Jonas's metaphysics offers a non-theological interpretation, based on the premise of an inner teleology of evolution, of the idea of Creation in the Jewish and Christian traditions. He clearly affirms that modern ethics has to be secular, immanent, and autonomous without, however, being willing to dismiss the content of religious metaphors such as the creation of humankind in the image of God. Instead, he seeks to rescue these metaphors, employing them in symbolic shorthand for the existence of a "sacred" dimension of life, which can make a compelling case for an ethics of responsibility without anchoring it in the notion of transcendence or in any "positive religion" such as Judaism or Christianity.[49]

If Jonas's task was, as Wiese puts it, to integrate the ideas of a Jewish theology of Creation on "the dignity and sanctity of life into a modern philosophical-ethical approach based on pure reason,"[50] then to what extent is his ethics really devoid of dependence on theological notions? It is the tacit presence or ontological priority of theology (notably the notion of the sanctity of creation) in Jonas's thought that enables us to undertake a deeper analysis of his work along with the biblical-Thomistic natural law tradition.

The Natural Law and Hans Jonas

At first glance, it would be easy to dismiss Jonas's work as falling outside the scope of this tradition—not merely because Jonas is a Jewish existentialist philosopher, but also because he is seemingly ambivalent about the need for theology when it comes to the ground of ethics. Indeed, Jonas seeks to ground a universal ethics in something *other* than Biblical or theological notions, arguing that obligation exists *within* all of value-laden being. Yet as I have sought to show, his thought retains an inherent openness toward the Divine. Jonas's Biblical-Jewish heritage imbues his philosophical thought with theological premises that, while not explicit or primary, are nonetheless vitally present, and it is this that renders his ethics amenable to a robust sense of the natural law. I will conclude by outlining three points of contact between Jonas's ethics and the natural law that remain to be developed.

The first point of contact is Jonas's work on the philosophy of the organism and of the interiority of nature. Modernity's inability to conceive of nature in an adequate sense (i.e., nature as having finality, form, and meaning), and hence an inability to see nature as symbolic of God, is why Jonas's concept of nature is extremely helpful, for he is trying to reclaim a notion that is neither Cartesian (dualistic) nor strictly materialist. His understanding of the inwardness of all living things as "pre-figuring" the freedom of the human spirit places his work alongside philosophers such as Kenneth Schmitz, Josef Pieper, and Robert Spaemann, whose work on the interiority of being retrieves the Aristotelian notion of form within a Catholic understanding of created *esse*. Much work needs to be done in articulating the meaning of *created* being and showing how this would augment Jonas's existentialist philosophy.

The second point of contact is Jonas's profound concern with revitalizing both ethics and man's sense of responsibility for his actions, especially in terms of protecting the environment and preserving the essence of man. There is a resonance, however dissimilar, between Jonas's understanding of responsibility and that developed by Karol Wojtyła.[51] Establishing and deepening the connection between freedom, responsibility, and especially truth would go a long way toward our understanding of the meaning of responsibility in a technological age. Furthermore, making the relation between ethics and theology explicit (via a created ontology) would aid in strengthening ethics.[52] Jonas's project seems to be a step in this direction.

The third point of contact is Jonas's "faith" or, at least, his openness to the Divine. In his memoirs, Jonas explains: "in earlier times [the Divine] used to illuminate everything [for me] but today is becoming increasingly difficult to believe in....Yet I'm profoundly convinced that pure atheism is wrong, that there's something more, something we can perhaps articulate only with the help of metaphors but without which being in all its facets would be incomprehensible."[53] As Stephen Kampowski puts it, "the question of whether God exists is not at all indifferent for our conduct," because "if the world were simply the product of the irrational, then moral action would be impossible. Life would be without reason or rhyme and no criteria for good or bad could be given."[54] Jonas's understanding of God, of the origin of the universe, and of the relationship between divine and human action needs to be clarified, for this would help illuminate Jonas's own reasoning concerning man's action, as well as bring to light areas in need of correction. Furthermore, a better understanding of the intrinsic relationship between reason and faith (philosophy and theology) is crucially needed in order to move forward in a dialogue between Jonas's philosophical ontology and a metaphysics of creation.[55]

There are many more questions that need to be put to Jonas's theory of responsibility. Yet his profound development of the sense in which "ontology necessarily entails a doctrine of obligation" is fruitful for a better understanding of the concepts of nature and responsibility operative in natural law—a contribution which still needs to be harvested and brought to fulfillment.[56]

Notes

1. Hans Jonas, *The Phenomenon of Life: Toward a Philosophical Biology* (1966; reprint, Illinois: Northwestern University Press, 2001), xxiii.
2. Hans Jonas, "Technology, Ethics, and Biogenetic Art: Observations on the New Role of Man as Creator," *Communio: International Catholic Review* (Spring 1985), 95.
3. John Finnis expresses his position as follows: "Natural law can be understood, assented to, applied, and reflectively analyzed without adverting to the question of the existence of God," because it depends upon an intuitive, simple non-inferential grasp of the good, wherein man spontaneously "grasps" the goods to be pursued, in *Natural Law and Natural Rights* (Oxford University Press, 1980), 49. See also 34-36.
4. Lawrence Vogel, "Natural Law Judaism?: The Genesis of Bioethics in Hans Jonas, Leo Strauss, and Leon Kass," *The Hastings Centre Report*, 36.3, (2006), 41, 43.

5. Christian Wiese, ed. *Memoirs: Hans Jonas,* trans. Krishna Winston (Massachusetts: Brandeis University Press, 2008), 202.
6. Hans Jonas, *Philosophical Essays: From Ancient Creed to Philosophical Man* (1980; reprint New York: Atropos Press, 2010), xiii. As Wiese states in *Memoirs,* 249: "Jonas's intellectual contributions…should, in the future, never be viewed separately from his own biographical awareness, rooted in his quintessentially Jewish twentieth-century experience." For a shorter synthesis of Jonas's intellectual biography, see Alan Rubenstein, "Hans Jonas: A Study in Biology and Ethics," *Society,* Vol. 46, Issue 2 (March 2009), 160-67. Jonas himself was acutely aware of the way in which his historical circumstances conditioned his thinking, as he states in *Philosophical Essays,* xii: "My apologia on the following pages is intellectual as well as biographical. The latter aspect cannot be avoided, as it tinges the former with that irreducible element of contingency from which a century like ours did not spare the life of the intellect." He is referring to Nazi Germany and the outbreak of the Second World War, which forced him to stop his work on Gnosticism, the topic of his doctoral dissertation. But he is also referring to his personal experiences, namely, having been a student of the greatest German intellectual of that time, Martin Heidegger. Jonas's philosophy of the organism is an attempt to correct the nihilism found at the core of Heidegger's existential interpretation of Being, which Jonas undertakes in his first book, *The Phenomenon of Life* (1966).
7. Jonas, *Philosophical Essays,* xiii-xiv.
8. Jonas, *Phenomenon of Life,* xxiii, emphasis added.
9. See Hans Jonas, "Evolution and Freedom: On the Continuity among Life-Forms" (1984) in Lawrence Vogel, ed., *Mortality and Morality: A Search for the Good after Auschwitz* (Illinois: Northwestern University Press, 1996), where he states on page 69: "Whether we give this inwardness the name of feeling, receptiveness or response to stimuli, volition, or something else—it harbours, in some degree of 'awareness,' the absolute interest of the organism in its own being and continuation." Thus, inwardness does not exclusively mean rational subjectivity or self-consciousness, but is rather the inner dimension proper to all living being, by which it communes with its external environment. Elsewhere, Jonas explains that matter organized itself in such "a gradual assent from apparently unconscious organisms to more and more obviously conscious ones, [which] suggests that there is an essential connection between mode of organization of matter…and degrees of inwardness or presence of a subjective dimension." See Harvey Scodel, "An Interview with Professor Hans Jonas," *Social Research* 70, no. 2 (2003): 351.
10. *Mortality and Morality,* 63. Jonas's careful explanation of the emergence of mind (man's self-consciousness) from matter seeks to be monistic without collapsing the distinction between the two. He treats this idea in his 1988 essay, "Matter, Mind, and Creation: Cosmological Evidence and Cosmogonic Speculation," in *Mortality and Morality,* 165-97, which we cannot delve into here.
11. For Jonas, being (existence as such) bears value by virtue of its purposive existence in the face of non-being or nothingness. This he calls "a fundamental self-affirmation of being, which posits it *absolutely* as the better over against nonbeing," and draws this conclusion: "Hence, the mere fact that being is not indifferent toward itself makes its difference from nonbeing the basic value of all values, the first 'yes' in general," in *The Imperative of Responsibility: In Search of an Ethics for the Technological Age*

(Chicago: University of Chicago Press, 1984), 81.

12. *Phenomenon of Life*, 283.
13. Richard Wolin offers a somewhat sarcastic comment on this: "In Jonas's view, so formidable and potent have the new technologies at humanity's disposal become that they have rendered obsolete 2,500 years of ethical discourse." See Wolin, *Heidegger's Children: Hannah Arendt, Karl Löwith, Hans Jonas, and Herbert Marcuse* (Princeton University Press, 2015), 117. Jonas explains his reasons for the need for a new ethics in *The Imperative of Responsibility: In Search of an Ethics for the Technological Age* (Chicago: The University of Chicago Press, 1984), 1-22. For a summary of these reasons, see Stephen Kampowski, *A Greater Freedom: Biotechnology, Love, and Human Destiny (In Dialogue with Hans Jonas and Jürgen Habermas)* (Oregon: Pickwick Publications, 2013), 66-68.
14. *Mortality and Morality*, 54.
15. "A philosophy of mind comprises ethics—and through the continuity of mind with organism and of organism with nature, ethics becomes part of the philosophy of nature." He continues, "Only an ethics which is grounded in the breadth of being, not merely in the singularity or oddness of man, can have significance in the scheme of things." See *Phenomenon of Life*, 282, 284.
16. *Mortality and Morality*, 100, emphasis added. For a discussion of how Jonas takes Kant's categorical imperative ethics and transforms it into an ontological ethics, see Peter Wolsing, "Responsibility to Nature? Hans Jonas and Environmental Ethics," *Nordicum-Mediterraneum* 8, no. 3 (2013): B4.
17. *Mortality and Morality*, 102, emphases original. A question arises: What exactly would this responsibility entail? If all being is value-laden, are there degrees of responsibility, for instance, to our fellow men, to our families, that are stronger than our responsibility to strangers, or is Jonas illustrating the profound sense in which we are responsible for all our fellow men—being "our brother's keeper?" How would the limits of this responsibility be worked out, if any? What does this entail for our responsibility to animal and plant life, and that too in its varying degrees of animation? Is our responsibility absolute? This "absolute" aspect is one of Wolin's objections to Jonas: that the parent-child paradigm is non-universalizable. See *Heidegger's Children*, 122.
18. Hans Jonas, "The Concept of Responsibility: An Inquiry into the Foundations of an Ethics for Our Age" in Daniel Callahan and H. Tristram Engelhardt, Jr., eds., *The Roots of Ethics: Science, Religion, and Values* (New York: Plenum Press, 1981): 59, 70; see also *Imperative*, 39, 101, 130-135. Jonas specifies that the duty toward children and the duty toward later generations are not the same thing—he takes up the important differences in *Imperative*, 38-46. Many object to this paradigm of responsibility; see Richard Bernstein, "Rethinking Responsibility," *Hastings Centre Report* 25, no. 7 (1995): 13-20.
19. *The Roots of Ethics*, 70.
20. *Imperative of Responsibility*, 44. See also *Mortality and Morality*, 100-101. Henry Veatch's response regarding the naturalistic fallacy is strikingly similar; see "Natural Law and the "Is"-"Ought" Question: Queries to Finnis and Grisez," in *Swimming Against the Current in Contemporary Philosophy* (Catholic University of America Press: 1990), 302-303.
21. *Mortality and Morality*, 101.

22. Vogel, "Natural Law Judaism?", 32.
23. Ibid, 34.
24. Ibid, 35.
25. "Though external teleology (the view that nature is God's creation) may be grafted onto an internal teleology, there is no need to ground metaphysics in theology." See Lawrence Vogel, "The Outcry of Mute Things: Hans Jonas's Imperative of Responsibility" in David Macauley, ed., *Minding Nature: The Philosophers of Ecology* (New York: Guildford Press, 1996), 179.
26. Vogel, "The Outcry of Mute Things," 178.
27. *Philosophical Essays*, xvii.
28. *Phenomenon of Life*, 284.
29. *Philosophical Essays*, xvii.
30. *Mortality and Morality*, 102.
31. Ibid, 101.
32. While some scholars, as well as Jonas's wife Lore, classify his work into three categories—gnosticism, organism/philosophical biology, and ethics/technology—the theological has also been noted as a fourth aspect of his philosophical corpus (as Lawrence Vogel does in *Phenomenon of Life*, xiv). Kampowski names this fourth category "cosmogonic speculations and theodicy" in *A Greater Freedom*, xvii. See Scodel, "An Interview with Professor Hans Jonas," 339.
33. Eric Lawee argues that insistence on the particular *Jewish* dimensions in Jonas's thought "can easily lapse into exaggeration," for these elements are dominantly biblical (mainly from the Book of Genesis) and are therefore Judeo-*Christian* rather than strictly Jewish sources. See Eric Lawee, "Hans Jonas and Classical Jewish Sources: New Dimensions," *Journal of Jewish Thought & Philosophy* 23 (2015): 108. Lawee concludes Jonas was "in essence, a philosopher who happened to be Jewish rather than a philosopher of nature whose work was informed by Judaism," and that it is his biblical heritage rather than a post-biblical Judaism that is resonant in his thought; see Lawee 117-18.
34. *Phenomenon of Life*, 283.
35. *Mortality and Morality*, 201-202.
36. See "Concerning the Necessity of Metaphysics" in *Imperative of Responsibility*, 45-46. Vogel explains that "Jonas does not take theology to be necessary for an overcoming of nihilism. Rational metaphysics must be able to ground an imperative of responsibility without recourse to faith," and although theology is not *required* for an ethics rooted in metaphysics, it remains compatible with aspects of Judeo-Christian theology. See *Minding Nature*, 169, 182.
37. Even "minimalist" versions which are thoroughly teleologic, such as the Aristotelian natural law of Henry Veatch, do not account for the full context of natural law, ultimately remaining like one-winged birds. It is beyond the scope of this paper to present the elements needed for a proper Catholic natural law theory. For a good discussion of this, see Fulvio Di Blasi's *God and the Natural Law: A Rereading of Thomas Aquinas*, Trans. David Thunder (Indiana: St. Augustine's Press, 2006), which endeavours to return to the source where natural law theory was presented in an effort to dialogue with the current revival of NLT that is self-professedly independent from God's existence. Di Blasi states that the concept of natural law "points to God as the axiological foundation of the ethical order, and entails a moral view in which human action ultimately takes its

meaning from an *act of obedience,* out of love, to the order placed in things by God" on page 1. Put simply, natural law cannot be defended apart from the eternal law. To do so would be like uprooting a tree and artificially maintaining it, so it has the semblance of being alive, but is missing its essential connectedness to the context in which it exists and thrives. An "atheistic" natural law ultimately cannot account for the origin and *telos* of the world's being.

38. Christian Wiese, *The Life and Thought of Hans Jonas: Jewish Dimensions,* trans. Jeffrey Grossman and Christian Wiese (Massachusetts: Brandeis University Press, 2007), xv.
39. Vogel, "Natural Law Judaism?", 35. See also Wiese, *Life and Thought,* xxi.
40. Wiese, xix.
41. Ibid.
42. Ibid, 113.
43. Ibid.
44. Wiese, in Samuel Fleischacker, ed., *Heidegger's Jewish Followers: Essays on Hannah Arendt, Leo Strauss, Hans Jonas, and Emmanuel Levinas* (Duquesne University Press, 2008), 170. See also "Rotseh ba-hayyim—*Creation and Responsibility for the "Sanctity of Life"* in *The Life and Thought of Hans Jonas: Jewish Dimensions,* 102-120.
45. *Imperative,* 23, emphasis added.
46. *Philosophical Essays,* 181. Elsewhere Jonas says, "we must relearn to understand that there is such a thing as 'too far,' that the 'integrity of the human image' should be regarded as inviolable, and that 'we must rediscover fear and trembling, even without God, and awe of what is holy,' in "Technology, Ethics, and Biogenetic Art: Observations on the New Role of Man as Creator," *Communio* (1985): 106.
47. Wiese, *Heidegger's Jewish Followers,* 171. For instance, Wiese connects Jonas's concept of "the outcry of mute things" to "a terminology of creation…an attempt to draw the ethical consequences from his earlier philosophical speculations about organic life and to establish a profound metaphysical foundation for the inherent objective value of life." See *Life and Thought,* 105.
48. Wiese's argument that theology underlies Jonas's work from the beginning is in contrast to Vittorio Hösle's view that Jonas "appended" a theological dimension to his ethics in a later phase of his work. Wiese explains: "Jonas's own testimony, however, seems to point to a far more complex relationship between the philosophical and the Jewish component in his thought, one that cannot simply be defined chronologically in terms of a succession of subsequent phases of his work, but which rather overdetermines his entire work." See Hava Tirosh-Samuelson and Christian Wiese, eds., *The Legacy of Hans Jonas: Judaism and the Phenomenon of Life* (Brill Academic Publications, 2010), 423.
49. Wiese, *Heidegger's Jewish Followers,* 172.
50. Ibid, 175.
51. Karol Wojtyła / John Paul II is not the only Christian thinker to discuss responsibility (i.e. there is also Romano Guardini in *Power and Responsibility: A Course of Action for the New Age,* first English translation, 1961), but Wojtyła's understanding of being as gift is immensely helpful in developing an adequate notion of responsibility. In words highly similar to those of Jonas, Wojtyła writes: "Responsibility is, as it were, the culmination and necessary complement of freedom," and adds that a person cannot say "I am free" without also saying "I am responsible" to God and to others, as cited in

David L. Schindler and Nicholas J. Healy, eds., *Freedom, Truth, and Human Dignity: The Second Vatican Council's Declaration on Religious Freedom* (Eerdmans Publishing, 2015), 49. What is missing in Jonas is the intrinsic relationship between freedom and truth, and this must be developed.

52. Wiese notes Gershom Scholem's critique of secular foundations of ethics (like that of Jonas, even though Scholem was not directly writing in response to him): "The secularizing talk of the 'sanctity of life' is a squaring of the circle. It smuggles an absolute value into a world which could never have formed it out of its own resources, a value pointing surreptitiously to a teleology of Creation which is, after all, disavowed by a purely naturalistic rationalistic view of the world." See *Life and Thought,* 156.
53. *Memoirs,* 218. Wiese states: "Even if he was admittedly not at all a believer in the traditional sense… the alternative of atheism or even of merely distancing himself from Judaism appeared unthinkable to him." See *Life and Thought,* 152.
54. Kampowski, *A Greater Freedom,* in 78n55, quoting Pope Benedict XVI: "The issue is whether reality originates by chance and necessity, and thus whether reason is merely a chance by-product of the irrational and, in an ocean of irrationality, it too, in the end, is meaningless, or whether instead the underlying conviction of Christian faith remains true: *In principio erat Verbum*—in the beginning was the Word" (7 September 2007 Address at Hofburg, Vienna).
55. Jonas mentions this without developing it further: "a rational or philosophical metaphysics isn't prohibited from formulating 'suppositions' about the presence of the divine in the world. It seems to me, rather, that philosophical ontology is allowed to leave room for the divine." See *Memoirs,* 218.
56. *Memoirs,* 202.

In Search of the Sources of Conscience: Joseph Rickaby's Eudaimonistic Deontology

Megan Furman

When defining "conscience," the *Catechism of the Catholic Church* turns to the words of John Henry Cardinal Newman:

> Conscience is a law of the mind; yet [Christians] would not grant that it is nothing more; I mean that it was not a dictate, nor conveyed the notion of responsibility, of duty, of a threat and a promise….[Conscience] is a messenger of him, who, both in nature and in grace, speaks to us behind a veil, and teaches and rules us by his representatives. Conscience is the aboriginal Vicar of Christ.[1]

That Newman's description receives approbation by the Church, however, fails to simplify the range of appeals to "conscience" that come from sources both inside and outside of her embrace. Newman's articulation fails, furthermore, to establish the grounds by which such appeals might be arbitrated. What is conscience, and whence does it derive? Does conscience comprise a sort of innate knowledge? Or is it, as Newman's words could imply, the voice of God or of an angel? If so, then how can one discern when appeals to conscience might be valid or invalid?

This article shall not aim to settle centuries of dispute surrounding these questions. Rather, it shall undertake a more modest but fundamental task, namely, to identify the valid sources of conscience and thereby to propose some means for evaluating appeals made in its name. Limited in scope, this discussion will not seek the foundations of conscience from the full range of perspectives on the issue; rather, it will draw upon the life of natural virtue as envisioned in the Aristotelian-Thomistic tradition. The justification for this choice is simple. An Aristotelian-Thomistic account of conscience seems to resonate most with individual experience to the extent that it recognizes in conscience some point of reconciliation between personal legislation and public mores. Furthermore, an Aristotelian-Thomistic account may be one of few, if not the only, that can ask and answer in sincerity wherefore appeals to conscience may be called valid or invalid. The tradition's ability to establish objective criteria depends in part upon the fact that for St. Thomas, conscience is a natural phenomenon, which is to say it does not require faith, although of course, apropos of his more comprehensive vision, faith may aid and sharpen it. As fundamentally natural, conscience is not in essence mysterious or impenetrable by human reason, even if it may be experienced as such. St. Thomas's philosophical treatment of conscience demystifies it just enough to disclose how, much like a virtue, conscience must be cultivated.

While one could undoubtedly gain insight into conscience from St. Thomas himself, the range of alternatives that have sprung up since his time, particularly in the modern era, may warrant some more direct engagement. For this reason, I have chosen to rely not primarily on St. Thomas, but rather on Joseph Rickaby, S. J., whose situation in the early twentieth century places him—philosophically speaking—at something of a helpful crossroads. The legacies permeating Rickaby's milieu, such as those of Bacon, Hobbes, Hume, Rousseau, Kant, and Hegel, to name a few, precipitated the need for him to take seriously and to address certain problems less immediate, if not foreign, to St. Thomas. That is not to say that St. Thomas may not have anticipated these problems, nor that his work offers no insight into them. Rather, the point is simply that Rickaby's explicit critiques of philosophical trends (see, e.g., his work *Scholasticism*) might be of greater immediate service to those in the contemporary world attempting to navigate the plethora of perspectives currently on offer.

In attempting to tease out the valid sources of conscience, this investigation ought to accomplish two intermediate tasks. First, by leaning heavily on Rickaby, it will need to clarify how the Thomistic tradition conceives of "conscience." Within the Thomistic framework, conscience finds itself entangled with the intellectual and moral virtues, most notably the virtue of prudence. And yet, as Rickaby points out, conscience is *not* a virtue, nor ought it to be confused with prudence. What is it, then, and how precisely does it relate to the virtues, whether prudence or otherwise? That question will prompt examination not only of conscience in relation to prudence, but prudence in relation to the moral virtues, which in turn will raise an apparently circular conundrum. According to Aristotle and his heirs, prudence presupposes moral virtue, but moral virtue presupposes prudence. How then can one grow in virtue, or, according to our broader argument, in conscience? Is virtue not somehow contingent upon circumstances outside of one's control? If so, then is conscience, too, merely a product of fate?

If one hopes to understand the mechanics by which conscience operates, then one shall also have to resolve this apparent circularity involved in prudence. What this article shall propose is that the kind of knowledge the Thomistic tradition calls "affective knowledge" can dissolve the dilemma, and so too, demystify the nature and the sources of conscience. Affective knowledge not only illuminates the mechanics of prudence, but further and perhaps more profoundly establishes the natural basis whereby we can evaluate appeals to conscience.

Nature and Conscience: The "Is" vs. the "Ought"

What is conscience? The context in which the term first shows up in *Moral Philosophy: Ethics, Deontology and Natural Law* serves not only to disclose Rickaby's answer but also to illuminate the alternatives popular in his historical context. Rickaby introduces "conscience" under the heading "Deontology," and the subheading "Of the Natural Law of Conscience." The attentive reader might find the combination curious: deontology and natural law? In this pairing, however, lies the heart of Rickaby's contributions.

As a prolegomenon to the "natural law of conscience," Rickaby finds it necessary first to assess what we mean by "nature." In what ways do we call the "natural law" natural? Drawing from Aristotle, Rickaby puts forth two uses of the word. A thing may rightly be called "natural," he asserts, first, because it belongs characteristically to a species. "Whatever is found in all the individuals of a kind,"

Rickaby explains, "is taken to belong to the specific nature, or type of that kind." Something is "natural," in other words, if it is proper to the form or essence of a thing. A formal definition alone, however, seems insufficient; thus Rickaby complements the former with appeal to final cause. A thing may additionally be called natural, therefore, insofar as it is a thing "which any rational nature must necessarily compass and contain within itself in order to arrive at its own proper perfection and maturity."[2] Unsurprisingly, Rickaby's definition of what is "natural" corresponds to Aristotle's twofold perfection of a thing, by reference, firstly, to integrity of specific form, and secondly, to teleological fulfillment. According to Rickaby, then, and to his Aristotelian-Thomistic inheritance, to be "natural" means to be necessary for the perfection of one's nature.

If by "natural" we mean necessary to the perfection of one's nature, then the natural law acquires weight in the context of ethics. In other words, it will be necessary to my very happiness not only to know the natural law but to abide by it. How, though, am I to achieve each of these tasks? Obviously my circumstances will require not only that I know general principles of the law, but also can determine their particular application. According to Rickaby, this demand constitutes the domain of conscience:

> It is proper to a free and rational being to guide itself, not to be dragged or pushed, but to go its own way, yet not arbitrarily, but according to law. The law for such a creature must be, not a physical determinant of its action, but a law operating in the manner of a motive to the will, obliging and binding, yet not constraining it: a law written in the intellect after the manner of knowledge: a law within the mind and consciousness of the creature, whereby it shall measure and regulate its own behaviour. This is the natural law of conscience. It is the Eternal Law, as made known to the rational creature, whereby to measure its own free acts.[3]

Here, then, we have entered the realm of conscience. Conscience, he says, is a law, a law which is both natural and eternal; it is man's participation in the eternal law. Rickaby's formulation conforms thus far to that of his Thomistic inheritance. In a naturalistic bent, he continues, conscience is

> a practical judgment of the understanding. It is virtually the conclusion of a syllogism, the major premise of which would be some general principle of command or counsel in moral matters; the minor, a statement of fact bringing some particular case of your own conduct under that law; and the conclusion, which is conscience, a decision of the case for ourself according to that principle.[4]

One can discern in Rickaby's emphasis on nature the intent to wrest conscience out of the hands of sentimentalists and utilitarians, and thus to counter the variety of rival conceptions influenced by, for example, Hutcheson, Hume, Bentham, and Mill. "We refuse to acknowledge," Rickaby insists, "any Moral Sense, distinct from Intellect. We know of no peculiar faculty," he continues, "specially made to receive 'ideas, pleasures and pains in the moral order" (Mackintosh, *Ethics*, 206). "Most of all," Rickaby goes on:

> We emphatically protest against any blind power being accredited as the organ of morality. We cannot accept for our theory of morals, that everything is right which warms the breast with a glow of enthusiasm, and all those actions wrong, at which emotional people are prone to cry out, *dreadful, shocking*. We cannot accept emotions for arbitrators, where it most concerns reasonable beings to have what the Apostle calls "enlightened eyes of the heart" (Eph 1:18), that we may "know to refuse the evil and to choose the good." (Is 7:15)[5]

Does Rickaby's reaction to modern sentimentalism lead him to divorce conscience from the emotions and to identify it with a pure act of practical reason? In other words, if Rickaby speaks of conscience as the conclusion to a syllogism of practical reasoning, should it be conceived as an intellectual virtue in its own right? Rickaby considers and explicitly denies that equation, distinguishing conscience from the virtues as an *act* as opposed to a *habit*. Following Aquinas,[6] Rickaby aims to preserve especially the distinction between conscience and synderesis, the latter of which, and not the former, he characterizes as a habit. Synderesis, he clarifies, stands to conscience as cause to effect. Synderesis therefore serves as the first principle of the act of conscience while nevertheless remaining logically distinct. On the latter point, in fact, Rickaby insists more strongly than Aquinas. Whereas Rickaby carefully disentangles the two, Aquinas grants some leeway:

> Wherefore, properly speaking, conscience denominates an act... since habit is a principle of act, sometimes the name conscience is given to the first natural habit—namely, "synderesis"....For it is customary for causes and effects to be called after one another.[7]

Aquinas's explanation clarifies the difference between a colloquial and a philosophical use of "conscience." Rickaby's, by contrast, formulated in an era in which alternatives may have held greater sway, underscores the difference between the former and the latter in order to account for the intelligent agency required by every single moral action. In other words, habit (e.g., synderesis) cannot be sufficient in determining a particular course of action. Habit disposes a person to act in a certain way, but one must intelligently deliberate a particular course of action given each particular situation. It is the product of such deliberation that Rickaby calls "conscience."

By addressing conscience in conjunction with natural law, Rickaby precludes the possibility of relativizing good and evil, right and wrong, in ways that might follow logically from philosophies based upon, for example, a moral "sense" or faculty. Instead, he attributes to conscience the ability to reason practically in moral matters. But does that mean that conscience is *merely* practical reason? In other words, does Rickaby's conception in effect concur with Kant's? To answer in the affirmative would be not only to overlook the essence of Aristotelian ethics, but moreover, to misunderstand the heart of Rickaby's project.

Reconceiving Ethics: The "Ought" that Grounds the "Is"

Like others of his time, Rickaby witnessed the social and political consequences of the Enlightenment that most would call problematic; unlike many of his contemporaries, however, Rickaby traces the source of these problems not to one or another kind of structure, but rather to the premises of the modern project as a whole. In other words, Rickaby sees at the root of modernity a fundamentally flawed understanding of "nature." It is precisely for this reason that *Moral Philosophy* begins by clarifying this term. Importantly, however, Rickaby does not intend to end with "nature," for even that principle proves insufficient in establishing what Rickaby perceives as an adequate philosophy. If nature were sufficient, then Rickaby would not so unflappably critique the very thinker to whom his tradition is indebted. But critique he does. Unabashedly referring to his forebear, albeit with all due respect, as an "imperfect Moral Philosopher," Rickaby intends to illuminate where Aristotle comes up short, and—more importantly—to make up for that deficiency. What he considers lacking in Aristotle is, in some ways, the same answer to the modern problem of the "is" and "ought:" "For if the principal business of Ethics is to determine what moral obligation is, then the classical work on the subject, the *Nicomachean Ethics* of Aristotle, is as the play of *Hamlet* with the character of Hamlet left out: for in that work there is no analysis of moral obligation, no attempt to fix the comprehension of the idea I *ought*."[8]

Rickaby's rendering of the is–ought problem must be carefully evaluated, however, for it does not quite parallel the question as most moderns would pose it. As Rickaby construes the issue, a "system of Eudaemonism" may impinge upon the deliberations of a person who cares about his or her own happiness, but it will have little or nothing to offer one who does not consciously seek to fulfill his *telos*. "Any man," writes Rickaby, "who declares that he does not care about ethical or rational happiness, stands to Ethics as that man stands to Music who 'hath no ear for concord of sweet sounds.'" In other words, ethics as a rational enterprise lacks a motivating principle. While ethics can certainly "point out" happiness and claim that happiness comprises a person's sovereign good, if one remains unmoved, Rickably concedes, "Ethics can have no more to say."[9]

To an extent, Rickaby's formulation of the problem resonates with ancient disputes concerning the nature of knowledge and virtue. Rather than invoking the affective aspects of Aristotelian virtue to resolve the dilemma, however, Rickaby takes a different tack. His primary interest seems to lie in pointing out the inadequacy of Aristotle's natural teleology—if not in practice, at least in theory. To that end, Rickaby points out that no science can itself demonstrate its end. That end must be given externally. Thus ethics, considered as a science, cannot demonstrate the goodness of its proper end, which is to say, happiness. Where, then, shall this end be obtained?

As Rickaby sees it, a coherent and comprehensive moral philosophy, not to mention a moral life, hinges upon the link between the "is" and "ought," the latter of which, in particular, remains elusive to Aristotle. It is the "ought," then, for which Rickaby especially intends to account in his renovated vision, which entwines both ethics and deontology:

> Moral Philosophy is divided into Ethics, Deontology, and Natural Law. Ethics consider human acts in their bearing on human happiness; or, what is the same thing, in their agreement or disagreement with man's rational nature, and their making for or against his last end. Deontology is the study of moral obligation, or the fixing of what logicians call the comprehension of the idea *I ought*. Ethics deal with *to deon*, "the obligatory." Deontology is the science of Duty, as such.[10]

Lest the reader of a Thomistic bent balk at the thought of a neo-Thomist embracing deontology of the Kantian variety, one need only look more closely at Rickaby's unique interpretation. Deontology takes center stage only as a complement to "happiness," which remains the primary concern of ethics and forms the primary building block of a comprehensive moral philosophy. In employing the vocabulary characteristic of the Kantian schools, Rickaby intends not to align himself with the former, but rather to modify or to reclaim "deontology" for the Scholastics. In Chapter VI, "Of the Origin of Moral Obligation," Rickaby denounces the Categorical Imperative as "not merely deficient, but positively in error." Kant's system, Rickaby explains, awards the force of law to a precept uttered by a man's own reason, but such force is impossible. No law, he contends, can possess authority without jurisdiction, both of which require some distinction between lawgiver and subject. Insofar as it "undertakes to settle the matter of right and wrong without reference to external authority," the Categorical Imperative, Rickaby maintains, must be fundamentally flawed. A man's reason *is* an aspect of that man, not something other than he; thus "the dictate of reason, as emanating from within oneself, is not a law." Without a law, Rickaby contends, "there is no strict obligation." Thus "the whole theory of obligation is not locked up in the Categorical Imperative, as Kant formulated it."[11] According to Rickaby, Kant's system cannot properly be called deontological.

But with what purport does Rickaby lodge such a complaint? What does it matter if Kantian deontology is not in fact deontological? Moreover, on what basis can Rickaby claim that the very definitions of law and obligation imply external authority? Rickaby has already accused Aristotle of a similar infraction, namely, that in ordering ethics to the happiness of man, Aristotle makes of man his own authority. No appeal to a human nature, he has asserted, can establish external authority. Where else might such authority derive? For one whose philosophical vision admits of a God who reveals a law contiguous with nature, the principle of duty needed for a proper deontology comes simply from the law of God. "The full notion of what a man *ought*," writes Rickaby, "is what he *must do under pain of sin*." In case one is tempted to conceive of sin as a form of mere intellectual ignorance, Rickaby argues for an offense far more grievous. "Sin," he insists, consists in "more than folly, more than a breach of reason." If sin were merely a failure of reason, then all sin would essentially reduce to "philosophical sin," or, in other words, intellectual error. But "far worse than that," Rickaby claims, "has the sinner done." In offending against his own reason, he continues, the sinner thereby offends as well "against a higher Reason, substantially distinct from his, standing to it in the relation of Archetype to type, a Living Reason, *hepsychos logos* (cf. Ar., *Eth.*, V., iv., 7), purely and supremely rational."[12] Clearly Rickaby espouses a Christian vision; in offending the order of reason, one offends not only oneself, but also another: the living source of reason itself.

In establishing an external authority for ethics, Rickaby not only heightens the stakes of the moral life, but he also does more: he situates all of general ethics within a cosmic order, the foundation and standard of which is neither man nor merely human reason, but rather, the reason of God. Within this adjusted order, deontology takes up its place not as self-derived obligation, but rather as the science of duty that will conduce to human happiness and which harmonizes with God's law and the natural order. Rickaby therefore rearranges the scope of moral philosophy. "In the order of sciences," he asserts, "Ethics are antecedent to Natural Theology; Deontology, consequent upon it."[13] The remainder of his work *Moral Philosophy* implicitly, if not explicitly, reflects this structure; having established certain groundwork in ethics, Rickaby turns to deontology, mediating the transition precisely by appeal to his renovated natural order.

In the context of moral philosophy, is Rickaby right to be concerned with such notions as duty, law, and punishment? Or are these trivial inventions of a post-Kantian world? If one should incline toward the latter perspective, one need only recall that, according to Rickaby, outside of one's own self-fulfillment, Aristotelian ethics cannot account for the notion that one *ought* or *ought not* to do anything. "Deontology," claims Rickaby, "not Ethics, expounds and vindicates the idea, *I ought*. [Deontology] is the science of Duty."[14] But again, why introduce duty? Is duty necessary to a moral life? The answer, for Rickaby, can be measured not by theoretical soundness, but by empirical evidence, which is to say, investigation into real human experience. To evaluate the place of duty in the moral life, therefore, we will turn to the development of virtue and the place of conscience in that process.

The Development of Virtue and Conscience

Having established the distinction between ethics and deontology as an internal versus external regulation; having identified the particular kind of external regulation of interest to his moral philosophy as the law of God, i.e., eternal law; the question remains: how does one come to know and act in relation to that external, eternal law? For Rickaby, any act involved in moral deliberation and action begins in the same sources as any other act of human knowing: "Primary moral judgments," he asserts, "arise in the intellect, by the same process as other beliefs arise there in matters of necessary truth."[15] Even with the spectre of the fact–value distinction looming over him, Rickaby does not shy away from the bold assertion. Rather, by embedding the source of moral authority in the same order of reason that sets the standard for scientific truth, Rickaby denies any cleavage between the two realms. The intellectual nature of conscience cannot, however, stand without defense, for after all, almost everyone recognizes some difference between the claims of a moral and, say, scientific order—everyone, that is, expect perhaps Kant, from whom Rickaby certainly desires to stand apart. What does Rickaby mean, then, when he claims that moral judgments arise in the intellect in the same manner as necessary truths?

The question raises controversy even among intellectualist sympathizers. Rickaby's articulation risks misconstruing the foundation of Aristotelian ethics and therefore ought to be unpacked. The stakes at issue may be illuminated by the criticism such a position has endured. One such critique comes from contemporary ethicist, Julia Driver, who objects to Aristotelian "intelligent virtue" on the basis that it limits virtue to a few, namely, "the wise." Driver argues:

> Virtue must be accessible—to those who are not wise but kind; to those who had the misfortune to grow up in repressive environments that warped their understanding, yet who are capable of showing the appropriate compassionate responses to human suffering.[16]

It is worth identifying more extensively two of Driver's main objections to an Aristotelian account. First, as Driver sees it, wisdom and understanding may not intrinsically pertain to kindness, or to compassion, for that matter. Instead, wisdom and understanding seem to describe specific kinds of intellectual acuity divorced from the emotional demands proper to interpersonal affairs. Second, according to Driver, wisdom and understanding seem to be less accessible than kindness or compassion. For that reason, an account of virtue based on intelligence may limit virtue to an elite few. Driver's concerns target one such as Rickaby, who writes, after all,

> As moral virtue is a habit of appetite, rational or irrational, a formation resulting from frequent acts…so the springs of conscience are certain intellectual habits, whereby the subject is cognisant of the principles of natural law, and of their bearing on his own conduct, habits which, like the habits of moral virtue, require to be formed by acts from within and succour from without, since merely the rudiments of the habit are supplied by nature.[17]

The formulation renders Rickaby vulnerable to accusations of "intellectual elitism," on the grounds that, if one must be intelligent to have a sound conscience, then some—namely, the less intelligent—are at a disadvantage. Is such an interpretation, however, fair to Rickaby or to his tradition? The next section will contend that critiques such as Driver's target a view of wisdom foreign to the Aristotelian tradition, and therefore, too, to Rickaby. To criticize Aristotelian virtue—or conscience, for that matter—on the grounds employed by Driver is to misunderstand the way in which intelligence informs each. As one familiar with Aristotle might expect, the fundamental wisdom demanded by moral virtue is practical, not speculative, in nature. The natural intelligence required by Rickaby pertains not to intellectual acumen per se but to intelligent appraisal of human affairs. Such intelligent appraisal, moreover, inherently involves the emotions, grounding—in some cases—responses such as compassion and kindness, and thereby, too, establishing the standard or measure for all appeals to conscience.

Natural Sources of Virtue and Conscience: Affective Knowledge

In Rickaby's tradition, the wisdom pertaining to moral virtue is classified as *phronesis*, or prudence, defined in the *Nicomachean Ethics* as "right reason with respect to things to be done." Listed alongside of *techne*, *episteme*, *nous*, and *sophia* as a quality "through which the mind attains truth in affirmation or denial,"[18] prudence falls among the intellectual, rather than the appetitive, virtues. Nevertheless, its particular taxonomy remains distinctive. Insofar as it deals with action, prudence requires the power to command the other faculties to execute an action in accord with its ordinance. Moreover, since the power to command is appetitive in nature, prudence must also involve the appetites. The appetitive aspect will be taken up in due course; more immediately, however, it is worth noting that in Book X, Aristotle further complicates its mechanics. Relating prudence to moral virtue not strictly as a ruler to one ruled, but as dependent upon the latter, as well, Aristotle states: "Prudence too is connected with moral virtue, and moral virtue with prudence since the principles of prudence are taken from the moral virtues and the rectitude of the moral virtues from prudence."[19] Has Aristotle not created a circular conundrum? To restate the problem more plainly: If moral virtue requires prudence and prudence requires moral virtue, which comes first? The remainder of this section will aim to show how the apparent circularity involved in prudence is resolved through a proper understanding of the particular kind of knowledge involved in moral matters, a kind of knowledge, moreover, which serves both to defend intelligent virtue and to establish the valid sources of conscience.

Aristotle remains notorious within his own tradition for the role he allows a kind of knowledge often called "knowledge by experience." Such is the knowledge presupposed of the proper student of the *Nicomachean Ethics*. While Aristotle himself fails to comment systematically upon this kind of knowledge, his heirs take up the task in his wake. Late members of the tradition, in particular, focusing on the affective, rather than conceptual, aspect of this knowledge, duly render it "affective knowledge."

Affective knowledge, as all knowledge, begins with a sensitive experience of the world. It is distinguished, however, from conceptual knowledge by the way in which the intellect works upon a sense impression. In other words, whereas an epistemology of conceptual knowledge considers how a sense impression is received into the common sense, the imagination, and so on to the passive intellect, a look at affective knowledge considers how the very same sense stimulus elicits embodied responses.[20] Affective knowledge is therefore always involved in a particular subject's experience of an object as good or bad, pleasing or displeasing, perhaps even beautiful.[21]

Importantly, however, affective responses, considered independently, do not themselves constitute knowledge. To become proper knowledge, the information furnished by one's affects must be grasped in an act of the intellect. As Rickaby himself points out in staged dialectic, for the affects to produce knowledge requires a certain mechanics that reaches its fulfillment only in reflection. "'However does he get to know what *right* and *wrong* are?'" Rickaby prompts. "'Surely sensory experience cannot teach him that.' We answer, man's thoughts begin in sense, and are perfected by reflection."[22] This understanding of affective knowledge represents a development to the thought of Aristotle, albeit not one unique to Rickaby.

The intelligent nature of affective knowledge implies that throughout one's life, one continually adds to and reflects upon one's store of moral knowledge as one brings it to bear upon new situations. One may commit an act of injustice and come to observe the detrimental effects of the error; alternatively, one may suffer injustice and, by reflection, judge what the just act could have been. Virtue develops through an integrated process in which reason permeates every mode of knowledge and by which one changes one's behavior in light of the knowledge one acquires. One sifts and orders principles in deliberation, evaluates the level of success or failure, and considers what was done well or could have been done differently. One enjoys the goodness or despairs of the evil that comes of an action and desires to bring the increased degree of moral knowledge to bear upon the next situation.

Taken in conjunction with conceptual knowledge, affective

knowledge provides a complementary and more robust understanding of the way in which we as intellectually-permeated, affective, and sensitive beings come to know the world, developing the raw materials upon which prudence operates. What is just and unjust, temperate and intemperate, even good and bad, must be learned amidst observation of the ways in which another's actions affect me, or mine affect another, or—in the case of vicarious experience—another's affect others.[23] The claim is a bold one, suggesting not merely that moral virtue involves knowledge and appetite, but rather that the very moral knowledge we bring to bear on moral deliberation—which is to say, the knowledge that informs conscience—derives from affective knowledge.

It is the affective nature of moral knowledge that alone can resolve the apparent circularity involved in prudence. If moral knowledge is gained in and through appetitive acts, then the appetites already accord with the knowledge that develops from the information they provide. On the one hand, one can see how prudence relies on the moral virtues: Prudence, "right reason," must derive from reliable affective responses. On the other hand, however, the moral virtues rely on prudence: Prudence specifies both their ends and their means. Elicited by an appetite inclined toward a good end, prudence determines the appropriate means and commands the act, summoning the support of the appetites and thus reinforcing their rectitude in accord with its dictate. The results of the entire act, then, processed intellectually as "good" or "bad," to what extent and why, integrate into one's moral knowledge and lie in wait until summoned to illuminate a future situation.

Lingering Problems: Prudence, Conscience, and Supernatural Influence?

Having identified the sources of prudence in the very same experiences that give rise to conceptual knowledge, but having distinguished the aspects under which these experiences are processed by intellect, it remains now to resituate conscience in light of prudence.

Recall that Rickaby, following Aquinas, treats conscience as a practical judgment of understanding that seeks to bring a particular case of one's own conduct under a moral principle, and to judge it according to that principle. Should such an act not simply be called a judgement of prudence or, more simply, *synesis* (rectitude of choice; a "part" of prudence alongside of *euboulia,* i.e., rectitude in deliberation)? Indeed, to a good extent, perhaps conscience and synesis run parallel. Is there any reason to distinguish between them?

The remainder of this article will engage preliminary musings on the differences between synesis and conscience. If Rickaby defines "conscience" as the conclusion of a practical judgment of the understanding (but not of the will), then it seems that conscience may refer solely to the intellectual aspect of deliberation in moral matters and not to the appetitive aspect. Conscience may not, therefore, entail either affective knowledge or command. That conclusion would satisfy the distinction between synesis, the *virtue* of choosing well, and conscience, an *act* of practical reason conducted in light of moral principles. It would also mean, however, that taken in itself, conscience is neither (1) habitual nor (2) rightly ordered. The upshot is, of course, that conscience can err. This should come as no surprise since we refer to conscience as sound or unsound. But how does one determine the difference?

In treating conscience within a framework of both natural law and deontology, Rickaby offers the apparatus whereby we can establish criteria for appeals to conscience. As with promulgations of positive law, the dictates of conscience can be licit or illicit, in truth or in error. In other words, the very same order that measures conscience is that which measures all of reality, which is to say, the law of God. Appeals to conscience, therefore, can never trump the natural or eternal orders. Sound conscience refers to one's grasp of the law of God as it applies in one's particular circumstances.

Is that, however, the last word on the matter? In the *Summa Theologica*, St. Thomas considers another option: "Origen says [*Commentary on Romans* 2:15] that 'conscience is a correcting and guiding spirit accompanying the soul, by which it is led away from evil and made to cling to good.'"[24] Might conscience be, or come under the influence of, something supernatural? In case one is tempted to dismiss Origen's perspective as obsolete, one need only look to the Catechism:

> Conscience is a law of the mind; yet [Christians] would not grant that it is nothing more; I mean that it was not a dictate, nor conveyed the notion of responsibility, of duty, of a threat and a promise....[Conscience] is a messenger of him, who, both in nature and in grace, speaks to us behind a veil, and teaches and rules us by his representatives. Conscience is the aboriginal Vicar of Christ.[25]

Origen and Newman raise a real problem. Aristotle had no "conscience" apart from the natural act of practical judgment. Conscience is a Christian development. What, then, does conscience add to, or detract from, the basic act of moral judgment?

There are at least two answers to this question, the former simple, the latter more complex. Simply put, insofar as it is Christian, conscience allows for the influence of grace in the moral life. In other words, one who consults his conscience may judge that the action to be done is one which is, in fact, *super*human, e.g., to take a bullet for another, or—less dramatically—to hold his tongue when falsely accused; to extend mercy where justice would demand punishment; to adopt voluntary poverty as an act of faith in the providence of God. A life of conscience may be animated not only by natural virtues, but also by theological virtues and the gifts of the Holy Spirit:

> A lower principle of movement is helped chiefly, and is perfected through being moved by a higher principle of movement, as a body through being moved by a spirit. Now it is evident that the rectitude of human reason is compared to the Divine Reason, as a lower motive principle to a higher: for the Eternal Reason is the supreme rule of all human rectitude. Consequently prudence, which denotes rectitude of reason, is chiefly perfected and helped through being ruled and moved by the Holy Ghost, and this belongs to the gift of counsel, as stated above (Article 1). Therefore the gift of counsel corresponds to prudence, as helping and perfecting it.[26]

As grace reorders the human life to a new end, so too, in judging of the means toward that end, does Christian conscience.

The more complicated answer, however, concerns the kinds of sources that might factor into even a natural act of conscience. A person who accepts a supernatural order, for example, may naturally consult and give more weight to different kinds of sources than another who does not accept that order. They may include, for example, various moral opinions that one respects on authority, rather than from direct, affective experience. While both prudence and conscience judge of the means to a good end, conscience, to the extent that it accepts precepts known not directly but on authority, may alter the conception of the good to be pursued, and in pursuing, of the means most suited to that end. If the sources consulted by conscience include anything outside of human ken, then the good toward which it aims might likewise appear odd by human standards.

The risks associated with this position quickly become evident. If the sources of conscience may transcend human ken, and if appeals to these sources may yield actions idiosyncratic to the natural order, then how can society ever evaluate and regulate appeals made in the name of conscience? Rickaby provides the needed insight. In first naturalizing conscience, Rickaby denies the possibility that it operates by means of special access to the divine *as apart from* the natural order. In other words, conscience cannot first and foremost appeal to mysterious, esoteric, or primarily religious knowledge. Rickaby by no means intends to neglect the influence of grace, authority, and possibly even mystical communication in acts of conscience; he does intend, however, to protect the integrity of a cosmic order which is irrefutably rational. Sound conscience may therefore transcend, but it cannot violate, the natural order. The idiosyncrasies of actions carried out in light of conscience may be nobler—but never baser—than those which prudence would counsel.

Conclusion: Conscience and Its (Valid) Sources

As a modern thinker steeped in Thomistic thought, Joseph Rickaby can straddle traditions ancient, medieval, and modern. Rickaby's various works display an understanding of and appreciation for the scholastic tradition, in particular, combined with an objectivity necessary to critique it. While considered neo-Thomist himself, Rickaby does not shy away from reflecting upon the merits and limitations of his own tradition or from seeking to enhance it through the integration of others. To a backbone of medieval-scholastic thought, therefore, Rickaby adds compatible insights from the perspectives of modern science, Kantian deontology, and modern psychology.

In his self-critical adoption of Thomistic thought, Rickaby remains particularly cautious with regard to (1) legalism, and (2) *a priori* reasoning, both of which he attributes to scholastic thought more generally. His brand of Thomism, by contrast, not only admits of but prioritizes, in the line of modern science, close attention to empirical evidence. Rickaby views, moreover, the various domains of knowledge (e.g., astronomy, psychology, and metaphysics) as largely separate, rather than derivative. Such perspectives enable Rickably to distance himself from ideological commitments and thus to offer new formulations as he finds appropriate.

This review of Rickaby's thought ought not to imply unqualified endorsement. One might take issue, for example, with Rickaby's attitude toward the irreconcilability of first principles held by those with and without faith. Such discrepancies, however, need not detract from Rickaby's contribution. Regardless of how one thinks faith engages reason, Rickaby's account remains accessible. Its accessibility may in fact undermine Rickaby's own pessimism; so long as one can conceive of the possibility of divine law, *Moral Philosophy* offers an unpretentious description of the way in which divine law might interact with human reason in moral deliberation.

In rooting conscience in Aristotelian ethics complemented by a Christian deontology, Rickaby achieves for moral philosophy a blend of fixity and flexibility that none of his modern counterparts could offer. His synthesis harmonizes general, unchanging principles with more particular, contingent conclusions without compromising either the severity of divine law or the freedom of the individual. Conscience fits snugly into this vision. If, while not itself a habit, conscience remains grounded in one, then as any habit, conscience will demand different actions from different individuals. Diverse experiences and dispositions will inform diverse consciences in various ways. Nevertheless, conscience too, like virtue, will be measured by a standard of goodness. Consequently, conscience cannot be relative merely to one's own judgment. For Rickaby, the ultimate standard of conscience is the law of God; any accurate judgment of conscience will therefore conform to the former.

One can begin to see how conscience can be sound or unsound, and furthermore, that a sound conscience must be educated, trained, and developed in conformity with the natural order. Even among those of faith, Rickaby precludes the possibilities that conscience is a privileged faculty or a sort of innate gift or talent. In every person, the development of a sound conscience requires work; it begins with the cultivation of prudence, which in turn requires intelligent reflection upon affective experience and discipline of the appetites. The development of prudence, and of virtue more broadly, and of conscience for that matter, is *fundamentally* and *necessarily* human. Insofar as affective knowledge permeates the experience of every single intellectual, emotional, and sentient being in the world, so too will every such being have the aptitude to progress not only in moral virtue, but also in sound conscience.[27] Sound conscience depends upon and develops alongside the acquisition of virtue.

By rooting conscience in Aristotelian ethics, Rickaby avoids the risks associated with a purely rational, deductive moral science, such as that espoused by Kantian deontology. The affective nature of prudence and of the moral life, more broadly, shields Rickaby from strict intellectualism. So too do these natural roots in Aristotelian virtue, however, preclude sentimentalism and claims to privileged insight. Despite the fact that Rickaby fully embraces the influence of grace, he does not divorce conscience from the rule of natural law.

Instead, he aligns it precisely within that order, of which the eternal law serves as first and final principle. If conscience can transcend the natural law, it cannot violate the natural law; to do so would be to violate the eternal order. If conscience receives divine succour, then its dictate may produce an action that appears not to conform to the natural law of man (e.g., to preserve his life), but never in such a way that violates that law (e.g., to take his own life). The idiosyncrasy of an act inspired by supernatural influence cannot debase but only ennoble the human by revealing, through disclosure of his relationship to a higher-than-natural end, more fully *who he is*. Thus Rickaby establishes parameters for appeals to conscience. If the very purpose of conscience is precisely to preserve one's conformity with the natural and divine orders, then conscience must take its measure from the natural and eternal laws. An appeal to conscience will be valid insofar as its dictate conforms in the intricacies of one's particular situation to the law of God.

Rickaby's hierarchy of law and authority does not substantially differ from the broader thrust of the Thomistic tradition. What he may contribute uniquely, however, is a particularly insightful vision of the way in which nature and grace interact in the conscience of a believer. Unlike Newman, who in acknowledging the divine influence in conscience upholds the mystery of God's communication with us, Rickaby describes the more regular patterns of this communication, demystifying to an extent the relationship between grace and nature. That is not to say that he denies or naturalizes what his tradition affirms as mystery. Rather, Rickaby perhaps more clearly than any other captures the "naturalness" of the supernatural, or rather, its regularity or pattern. Accepting the Thomistic view that God is simple and unchanging, one can assume, like Rickaby, that, to an extent, so too are his ways. God will not, for example, inspire what in principle violates the natural or divine laws. As the influence of grace will uphold and elevate the moral virtues, so too will grace bolster and aid the work of conscience. In neither case will the effects of grace be unrecognizable; rather, by the fruits of grace will one know the tree.

Notes

1. *Catechism of the Catholic Church,* n. 1778; quoted from John Henry Cardinal Newman, "Letter to the Duke of Norfolk," V, in *Certain Difficulties felt by Anglicans in Catholic Teaching* II (London: Longmans Green, 1885), 248.
2. Joseph Rickaby, S.J., *Moral Philosophy: Ethics, Deontology and Natural Law* (London: Longmans, Green & Co., 1919), 134-35.
3. Ibid., 134.
4. Ibid., 135.
5. Ibid., 141. Italics are the author's. The citation given for Mackintosh contains the complete information provided by Rickaby; it is likely, however, that his source was James Mackintosh, *Dissertation on the Progress of Ethical Philosophy* (1830), prefixed to the seventh edition of the Encyclopædia Britannica.
6. Thomas Aquinas, *Summa Theologica* I, q. 79, a. 13.
7. Ibid.
8. Rickaby, *Moral Philosophy,* vi. Rickaby's use of quotation marks indicates that he is quoting from page 2 of his own volume.
9. Ibid. Rickaby's quotation comes from Shakespeare's *The Merchant of Venice.*
10. Ibid., 2.
11. Ibid., 70–71.
12. Ibid., 72.
13. Ibid., 8.
14. Ibid., viii.
15. Ibid., 140.
16. See Julia Driver, *Uneasy Virtue* (Cambridge, Cambridge University Press, 2001), 54; quoted in Julia Annas, *Intelligent Virtue* (Oxford: Oxford University Press, 2011), 30.
17. Rickaby, *Moral Philosophy,* 142.
18. Aristotle, *Nicomachean Ethics* VI,1139b.
19. Aristotle, *Nicomachean Ethics* X, 2112–2116.
20. For a thorough treatment see Richard Viladesau, *Theological Aesthetics: God in Imagination, Beauty and Art* (New York: Oxford University Press, 1999); or Francis J. Klauder, SDB, *Knowledge of the Heart: A Christian Epistemology: An Integrated Study of Human Knowledge* (Bangalore: Kristu Jyoti College, 1997).
21. But while we conceptually distinguish these paths, or kinds of knowledge, in reality we are gaining it all at once. For example, I experience a rose: I can see it, smell it, touch it and even taste it if I like; I know the rose as rose. But the concept of the rose leaves me with merely partial knowledge. I also know the rose as beautiful, its odor as pleasant; these observations have to do with the relationship between the rose and my affects or passions, and even my will (insofar as to know something as beautiful involves an act of the will, which delights merely in intellectual apprehension).
22. Rickaby, *Moral Philosophy,* 140.
23. For Aquinas, this is the role of *ratio particularis.* In "The Good, the Bad, and the Ugly: The Aesthetic in Moral Imagination," in *Beauty, Art and the Polis,* ed. Alice Ramos (Washington D.C.: American Maritain Association, 2000): 237-44, James P. Mesa develops a more colorful role for the "moral imagination" and points out the important role of the arts in this regard, insofar as through the arts—or simply by observing the actions of others around us—we can "virtually" inhabit those situations and gain

reliable moral knowledge.

24. Aquinas, *Summa Theologiae,* I, q. 79, a. 13, s.c. 1.
25. *Catechism of the Catholic Church,* n. 1778; quoted from John Henry Cardinal Newman, "Letter to the Duke of Norfolk," V, in *Certain Difficulties felt by Anglicans in Catholic Teaching* II (London: Longmans Green, 1885): 248.
26. Aquinas, *Summa Theologiae,* II-II, q. 52, a. 2, resp.
27. Annas, *Intelligent Virtue,* 65; see also 31 and 40. Indicating the difference between aptitude and circumstance, Annas points out that while we do not expect someone from the slums to become a maestro, it is not because he or she is incapable, but rather, that the opportunities for education are lacking. Responding more directly to the accusations of elitism issued by Driver, Annas suggests that Driver's objection actually proves the point, since Driver acknowledges gradations in virtue.

Equality and the Subversion of the Hierarchical Structure of the Natural Law

James Jacobs

Introduction

Patrick Deneen's 2018 book, *Why Liberalism Failed*,[1] sparked controversy because it maintains that the failure of liberalism is inevitable. Liberalism, he argues, is founded on an erroneous conception of the human person as an autonomous atom whose happiness lies in being liberated from every form of authority, be it natural, social, or religious. Deneen insists, however, that to free every person from all authoritative structures necessarily dissolves social relations and ushers in a moral relativism that empties life of spiritual significance. According to Deneen, the ubiquity of this experience of existential ennui in contemporary America is evidence that liberalism is in its death throes.

What might be surprising, though, is that his critique has also elicited objections from conservatives, for Deneen's argument also targets the American Founding's emphasis on individual freedom. Critics objected that Deneen fails to recognize that the thought of the American Founders relies on the tradition of natural law, and not a relativistic autonomy. For example, Robert Reilly, invoking John Courtney Murray's optimistic assessment of the Founding,[2] argued that the American doctrine of freedom tends not to moral dissolution, but rather encourages a community of religious and virtuous people.[3] Indeed, Reilly calls Deneen's argument a "suicidal blunder" which "demoralizes our youth and disarms us in the face of our enemies, who are further empowered by their disavowal of the founding." For Reilly, the great hope for Christian morality lies not in a wholesale attack upon the liberal freedoms of the American polity, but rather in recovering the truth of those founding principles in order save America from the perils of modernity.

This clash is simply the latest iteration of the long-disputed question of whether America is truly founded on the natural law.

I would like to address this anew, but with attention to two specific considerations. First, I believe that focusing too exclusively on the Founders and their principles obscures the issue, for if later developments have altered the *meaning* of those founding principles, subsequent generations are subject to that philosophical dislocation. In fact, I believe that the Founders themselves are somewhat ambivalent on natural law: while it is clear that many did embrace the tradition, it is equally clear that certain *seeds* of positions antagonistic to natural law are also present.[4] Regardless of what one believes of the Founders, though, I will argue that the way in which ideas developed in the nineteenth century did lead America away from the natural law tradition. Accordingly, Deneen might be wrong in saying our decline was inevitable from the start; but Reilly might be equally wrong in thinking we can simply recover unchanged the doctrines invoked by the Founders.

Second, while Deneen has rightfully indicted liberalism's idea of freedom, I would rather like to consider the corresponding element of Deneen's critique: liberalism's aspersion of authority in order to advance equality. I will argue that between the Founding and the Romantic era, the notion of *equality* evolved in such a way as to alienate America from the living principles of the natural law. The cause of this disaffection is that traditional natural law theory is based on a metaphysical principle that *difference implies hierarchy*, and so obedience to authority is necessary for the common good. The American tradition, embracing an unnuanced understanding of democracy, came to see the principle of equality as discrediting the notion of natural hierarchy and authority. This new doctrine asserts that *difference implies equality*, an innovation that replaces a natural deference to authority with an assertive individuality. This comes to be manifested in the American notion that all opinions are equal—they are merely different, not better or worse—thus eroding the very notion of moral authority, including the idea of objective moral truth. In this way, equality undermines the recognition of natural law as a standard of excellence for human life.

I will demonstrate this by showing, first, how traditional natural law theory embodies a hierarchical vision that permeates all orders of reality. I will then contrast this with the American creed of equality, which tends to obliterate recognition of authority. Finally, I will show how this difference is evident in society, since where a hierarchical society has an ordered unity, society without hierarchy becomes a multitude of disparate individuals in which diversity becomes an end in itself. Since such a society based on diversity can no longer recognize a common good, it is destined, as Deneen suggests, for dissolution.

Traditional Natural Law: Difference Implies Hierarchy

Let us begin by considering how traditional natural law necessitates respect for hierarchical authority. Thomas Aquinas defines the natural law as the participation of a rational creature in the eternal law.[5] The eternal law, in turn, is "the very Idea of the government of things in God the Ruler of the universe."[6] It follows that if God's creative act entails a hierarchy of beings ordered to the governance of the universe, the natural law would necessarily recognize these hierarchical relations as essential to justice and the common good of creation. The analogical nature of being, then, not only grounds metaphysical order in creation; it also is foundational for practical reason since hierarchical relations demand deference to authority. If the structure of reality reflects this hierarchical order, the democratic assumption that difference implies equality is not only metaphysically obtuse, but also anarchic with respect to practical reason's attempt to discern the order of a just society. To demonstrate this more clearly, let us consider how Thomas discovers the reality of hierarchy in metaphysics, in ethics, and finally in politics.

Metaphysically, the notion of hierarchical distinction among creatures is an essential element of Thomas's discussion of creation. For Thomas, creation involves not only bringing things into existence, but also the distinction between creatures and the orderly governance of that multitude.[7] Both of these latter aspects—distinction and governance—require a hierarchical ordering of nature.

First, the hierarchical distinction between creatures is a necessary corollary to the fact that God wills to create a variety of creatures.[8] God creates out of a gratuitous wish to share His goodness[9] but, because He is infinitely good,[10] this can only be adequately represented by a great multitude of creatures. Thus, Thomas argues that "goodness, which in God is simple and uniform, in creatures is manifold and divided and hence the whole universe together participates in the divine goodness more perfectly, and represents it better than any single creature."[11] However, since the act of existence (*esse*) received by creatures is the same creative act, the differentiation of created beings arises from the essences which receive existence. The various potentials of these essences limit being in disparate ways and so diversifies creatures. As Thomas explains, "Being itself, considered absolutely, is infinite; for it can be participated by an infinite number of things in an infinite number of ways. Hence if we take a thing with finite being, this being must be limited by some other thing which is in some way the cause of that being."[12] In other words, while all creatures exist, they differ from one another in the degree to which the potency of their essence enables them to possess existence by participation in *esse*.[13] This metaphysical principle of varying participations in the act of existence entails that *the creatures must be unequal*: some essences have greater potential to receive existence, and others have less. Nor is this inequality something invidious; rather, it is the only way for God to represent His infinite goodness: "In natural things species seem to be arranged in degrees....Therefore, as the divine wisdom is the cause of the distinction of things for the sake of the perfection of the universe, so it is the cause of inequality. For the universe would not be perfect if only one grade of goodness were found in things."[14]

Second, the universe is not perfected by the mere existence of diverse essences. Rather, since action follows from being, the diverse essences issue in a great variety of activities.[15] It is this diversity of activity that is the true goal of differentiation in creation. Indeed, Thomas says that things exist for the sake of their operations:

> Indeed, all things created would seem, in a way, to be purposeless, if they lacked an operation proper to them; since the purpose of everything is its operation. For the less perfect is always for the sake of the more perfect: and consequently as

> the matter is for the sake of the form, so the form which is the first act, is for the sake of its operation, which is the second act; and thus operation is the end of the creature.[16]

It is the cumulative activity of all these diverse creatures which together brings about the perfection of the universe. Therefore, God creates diverse grades of being so that they act in distinct ways to symbiotically benefit one another and attain the perfection of the universe. In fact, it is precisely in this mutually beneficial activity that creatures can be said to embody a likeness of God Himself. Thus, Thomas argues:

> Hence, the creature approaches more perfectly to God's likeness if it is not only good, but can also act for the good of other things, than if it were good only in itself....But no creature could act for the benefit of another creature unless plurality and inequality existed in created things. For the agent is distinct from the patient and superior to it.[17]

This is why creation, as a reflection of God's infinite goodness, must entail governance of creatures. The disparate activities of hierarchically distinct creatures must all be coordinated. This is precisely the effect of the eternal law,[18] God's providential governance of creation: "To providence it belongs to order things towards an end. Now after the divine goodness, the principal good in things themselves is the perfection of the universe; which would not be, were not all grades of being found in things."[19] These creatures are not only unequal, they are also symbiotically ordered to one another and so some beings are ordained to have superiority over others for the sake of the perfection of the universe. As Thomas says, "It is a greater perfection for a thing to be good in itself and also the cause of goodness in others, than only to be good in itself. Therefore God so governs things that He makes some of them to be causes of others in government."[20] The universe, then, is thoroughly hierarchical, and the great diversity of active powers can only attain perfection when the lower are subordinated to the higher.[21]

This hierarchical order of the macrocosmic universe is reflected in the soul of man, which as rational, enables man to represent that order microcosmically by understanding the perfection of the universe.[22] The soul, as a microcosm, must be hierarchically ordered itself if it is to realize its potential for perfection.[23] In his *Commentary on the Book of Causes,*[24] Thomas makes an interesting observation in support of the hierarchical superiority of the intellect over the other powers of the soul. Reflecting on the traditional neo-Platonic triad of being, living, and knowing, he notes that the higher powers have greater extension. Thus, being can be defined as what a substance has *in itself*, life is defined as a substance tending in activity *toward others*, but reason is defined by its ability to possess other beings intentionally, to bring other beings *into itself*. It is by virtue of reason that man can assimilate the order of the universe, to become virtually all reality.[25] That order, as participative in the eternal law, elicits obligations from man in return: as rational, he must effectuate that order by means of his activity. The rational ability to know that order thus becomes the basis for Thomas's ethical doctrines, for to reject the superiority of the intellect also is to ignore the providential order of creation. We can summarize the familiar ethical consequences of this psychic hierarchy: since man is defined as an intellectual creature whose soul virtually includes a variety of lower powers,[26] reason ought to control both the sensitive[27] and rational appetites,[28] since only those actions that manifest the fullness of rationality can be called good.[29] Conversely, any disruption of this hierarchical rule of reason is seen to be sinful,[30] since it is a privation of our intrinsic natural order to be rational *as well as* of the eternal law which ordains man to act rationally so as to bring about the perfection of the entire universe.[31]

Since man is a social being, the political order is the extension of this personal microcosmic order of goodness to the interpersonal nature of society. Hierarchical distinctions for the sake of the common good will therefore be crucial to any just political society. In the *De Regimine,* Thomas compares the polity to the universe and concludes that just as God orders all the parts of the universe in Providence, so all the parts of society ought to be ordered by the ruler.[32] In the first chapter of that work, Thomas neatly lays out why human society demands both authority and diversity, and so is naturally hierarchical:

> In all cases where things are directed towards some end but it is possible to proceed in more than one way, it is necessary for there to be some guiding principle, so that the due end may be properly achieved....One man...is not able to equip himself with all [goods requisite for life], for one man cannot live a self-sufficient life. It is therefore natural for man to live in fellowship with many others....If, therefore, it is natural for man to live in fellowship with many others, it is necessary for there to be some means whereby such a community of man may be ruled.[33]

His reasoning here mirrors the reasoning behind the metaphysical hierarchy of beings in creation. Since a perfect society requires a diversity of goods, different men must be given distinct vocations. Since, as with natures, a diversity of effects follows from a diversity of causes, this multitude of men can only attain a common good if there is a ruler who coordinates their activity. Crucially, just as is true of the universe, this obedience to authority is not for the benefit the leader, but for all in that well-ordered society.[34] To recognize this fact distinguishing authority from subordinates is in no way disrespectful, for all vocations are crucial for the common good. Nevertheless, some must have the unique vocation of exercising authority over others for the sake of coordinating activity for the sake of the common good. Elsewhere, Thomas suggests that this political hierarchy also reflects the order in the soul for he says that those who excel in reason ought to lead.[35] Reason, of course, grasps the order in nature, and so a reasonable authority would implement direction for the sake of the order of the eternal law. For this reason, all true laws must be based on the eternal law and the natural law.[36]

Some might object that this hierarchical division in society is an effect of the Fall. Thomas insists, though, that social distinctions are entirely natural and would have obtained even in the state of innocence, for even then man must be social, and it is natural that the man superior in wisdom and virtue should lead for the benefit of others.[37] Indeed, for Thomas this social inequality is part of the beauty of the cosmos as created by God: "The cause of inequality could be on the part of God...

[and] He would exalt some above others; so that the beauty of order would the more shine forth among men. Inequality might also arise on the part of nature as above described, without any defect of nature."[38] For this reason, obedience is an aspect of justice, since it is precisely what is owed to the superior by the inferior in any hierarchical order:

> In natural things it behooved the higher to move the lower to their actions by the excellence of the natural power bestowed on them by God: and so in human affairs also the higher must move the lower by their will in virtue of a divinely established authority. Now to move by reason and will is to command. Wherefore just as in virtue of the divinely established natural order the lower natural things need to be subject to the movement of the higher, so too in human affairs, in virtue of the order of natural and divine law, inferiors are bound to obey their superiors.[39]

It is important that our American ears not take too quick offense at this. This obedience is an aspect of justice because it is in accord with nature. Indeed, each person is created—the soul created by God and commensurated to the body in perfect hylomorphic unity[40]—for the sake of fulfilling a unique vocation in the order of providence.[41] The natural moral law commands that man conform to this order, thereby "being provident both for [himself] and for others."[42] An important aspect of fulfilling this providential order is to recognize one's place in the cosmic and social hierarchy and act according to the duties that follow from it; only in this way is each rendered that which is owed to him.[43]

Hierarchical Authority in the Natural Law

The practical importance of this hierarchical order is reflected in the fact that the precepts of the natural law explicitly note the need for obedience to authority. For Thomas, the primary precepts of the natural law are those follow self-evidently from that fact that man as rational "has a natural inclination to know the truth about God, and to live in society."[44] In other words, it is obvious that the teleological orientation of the rational creature is to grow in wisdom[45] and love[46] in communal intercourse with other men and, finally, toward God as the perfect embodiment of Truth and Goodness.[47] This truth grounds the other precepts of the natural law. The natural law then orders man to his end in two ways: firstly, in ordering the actions between men in temporal human society, wherein inquiry and friendship are realized; secondly, in ordering his relations to God as the eternal and infinite satisfaction of man's rational inclinations. Man's end is this two-fold happiness—temporal and eternal—ordered to perfecting his rational inclinations; the primary precepts of the natural law simply recognize this as the particularly human specification of the universal precept to do good and avoid evil.

Yet what must be done concretely to respect human society and to order oneself to God is not yet clear. For that reason, the primary precepts need to be augmented by the secondary precepts. These precepts, which Thomas identifies with the Decalogue,[48] specify the conditions for just relations with God and neighbor under which wisdom and love may flourish. What is noteworthy for our purposes is that the *first precept in each table of the Decalogue is a command to respect authority*. The first Commandment prohibits the worshipping of false gods, a corollary to which is to recognize the true and unrivaled sovereignty of Yahweh as Creator and Master of the universe.[49] The fourth Commandment, which Thomas sees to be parallel to the first, demands respect for worldly authority.[50] This deference to temporal authority includes piety both to our biological parents and also, because the family is an imperfect society, the rightly constituted authority in the perfect society of the polis.[51] The logic of both these precepts is that the first element of the common good is that obedience is owed to superiors; without the deference to the directive authority that coordinates diverse activities, society will dissolve in acrimony.

Let us take a moment to explain the necessity of hierarchical authority for the common good.[52] In a society composed of individuals with distinct duties and goals, each agent will naturally act on his own judgment about what is good for his own set of responsibilities.

However, if these disparate activities are to be coordinated, this multitude of individuals must yield to an authority, that is, they must defer to the judgment of someone who decides on the basis of what is best for everyone. This authoritative judgment is needed not just for material goods like punishing those who violate the peace or dividing the wealth accrued by society. More crucially, it is also required in order to foster spiritual goods like collective wisdom and love, for there must be someone to decide how common actions will be undertaken without causing division and acrimony. For example, even in the holiest of monasteries, there must be one person appointed as abbot in order to determine when all monks will gather for liturgies. If authority is a prerequisite for the common good, then hierarchy is natural, and obedience is necessary. As Yves Simon observes, this obedience is the virtue that recognizes one's own judgment is irrelevant in debates between oneself and the authority.[53]

Thus, just relations presume deference where it is called for. The fact that the first precept of each table concerns obedience well illustrates that natural law assumes hierarchical ordering in communities. For this reason, the common good is impossible without docility to authority. Without docility—the humility to subject one's actions to the authority of a superior—we can never learn to subordinate our subjective desires to the objective moral truth and the needs of the common good.

We must emphasize again that subordination in this order does not entail the denigration of the subordinate nor the rejection of human rights. All men are equal in their essential nature, and so are guaranteed all those rights needed to attain full human development. In order to attain that full human development, though, it is necessary that some must be subordinate to an authority who is given special prerogative to act for the common good on behalf of all. Indeed, those who obey benefit from the leadership of those who command, for this division of labor is necessary without prejudice to the value of the various offices. In fact, this hierarchical ordering is finally overcome, not in the order of justice, but in the order of charity, for it is in friendship that all men attain equality,[54] and the accidents of office are ignored in favor of the transcendent amity among all men.

Liberalism: Difference Implies Equality

Modern political liberalism is by nature antipathetic to hierarchy. Liberalism's central concern is to guarantee the maximal freedom and equality of persons in society.[55] As Deneen points out, the modern emphasis on equality demands that each person is empowered to determine his own end. This nullifies the role of authority in guiding people to a common end. One consequence of this is that justice needs to be reimagined: it is no longer realized in docilely accepting what one owes to others for the sake of the common good; rather, it is now reconceived in terms of rights held by individuals as claims against others in pursuit of their chosen end. Any assertion that one individual must be subordinate to another is to violate his right to self-determination and so can only be discriminatory and oppressive. If these are the effects of the doctrine of equality, it follows that even if the Founders invoked the natural law in constituting our political order, our nation will manifest a very different moral order than that held by the tradition at the time of the Founding.[56] This change is manifest in the evolution of America from the early nineteenth century: the more the American tradition came to sacrifice hierarchy for the equality of differences, the less it was able to bring cohesive unity to its multitude; the more the American tradition freed people from authority, the more cacophonous the chorus of rights claims became. Perhaps there is no more iconic expression of this than the famous lines from Walt Whitman, the poetic epitome of American Romanticism, who once offered this paean to his nation:

> Do I contradict myself?
>
> Very well, then, I contradict myself;
>
> (I am large—I contain multitudes.)[57]

Our question, then, is how did a people who justified their national identity on the basis of the hierarchical order of the natural law come to celebrate the contradictions and disorders of diversity begotten by an uncritical equality? Let us now consider some of the stages in this "progress" from an orderly social hierarchy to an egalitarian multitude.

The rejection of hierarchy, with the concomitant problematic nature of equality of differences, is implicit even in the origins of the nation. Ralph Barton Perry argues in his classic analysis of the intellectual character of the American founding, *Puritanism and Democracy*, that the Lockean natural law that is the immediate inspiration for the Founders eschews a reliance on the authority on God.[58] Instead of locating the natural law within the hierarchical order of the eternal law, Locke deduces it from his anthropocentric state of nature[59] in which each man is, as John Courtney Murray puts it, "a hard little atom in the midst of atoms equally hard, all solitary and self-enclosed… [who is] 'absolute lord of his own person and possession equal to the greatest and subject to nobody.'"[60] The version of natural law embraced in the Enlightenment is based not on the wisdom of divine authority but on brute human facticity. This utterly changes the orientation of natural law. As Perry observes, its precepts reflect the "limitations of mortal men," and so seek to enunciate only expedient rules conducive to merely "civil perfection." The natural law, then, is an instrumental "means to a human end" which is nothing but "the harmonious happiness of equal persons."[61] This harmony of equal agents is very different from an ordered unity dedicated to the perfection of human nature and the universe.

In fact, a significant precondition for accepting the equality of differences is that one must deny the metaphysical priority of truth and goodness. As one scholar has noted, "Locke's goal for society was the peaceful coexistence of citizens. For Locke, it was more important that each person in society follow his or her own conscience than for anyone to defend a doctrine of absolute truth."[62] The flattening of moral authority means the only basis for moral precepts is not God or reason, but the desire of these equal atoms. Once the priority of metaphysical truth has been obscured, the precepts of the natural law—what is owed to people—can no longer be derived from objective truth. This leads instead to a focus on the possession of individual rights with a rather murky derivation.[63] As Perry notes, since natural law is no longer found in the rational order of creation, "the doctrine of natural law and rights assumed the character of an uncritical acceptance of ready-made maxims…tinged with unconscious dogmatism" about what was "self-evident" to those proclaiming rights.[64] This lack of natural order also brings into question the grounding of political authority. If there is no objective basis for the common good, and if all moral opinions are equal, political authority is now reduced to hanging by that thinnest of threads, the consent of the people.

Because all desires are equal, a peculiar sort of egalitarianism based on compassion arises. In unconscious defense of their own self-interested desires, Americans will insist on the equality of every man to pursue his own end.[65] Historian David Wootton notes this break from tradition, for the "radical insistence that we are all motivated by exactly the same psychological and social drives and the political communities consist not of different types of people... but of people who are all fundamentally alike may usefully be said to mark the beginning of the Enlightenment."[66] In this way, the Enlightenment elevation of self-interest grounds tolerance: I tolerate your opinion because I will insist you tolerate mine; both opinions find common cause in being hostile to hierarchy, which would force the rejection of all inadequate opinions in favor of the truth. The first victim of the Enlightenment, then, is Christian natural law and its insistence on the objective nature of morality, since under the new regime the people are forced to accept as equal a great plurality of goods reflecting individual preference.[67] The seeds of Whitman's multitude are laid even before the Founding.

During the Revolution, those seeds take root. Thomas West claims in his book, *The Political Theory of the American Founding,* that "the foundation of [the Revolution] was the claim that all men are created equal….[This] had been discussed and embraced quite wittingly in America for more than fifty years [prior to the Revolution]."[68] In fact, equality is understood to be the justification for claims of political freedom: if all men are equal, they are equal in liberty, and so no one can take that liberty away. In short, as West argues, "Liberty means being left alone, not being coerced by others."[69] Liberty can thrive only in the absence of hierarchy, which is understood to be coercive. Consequently, giving primacy to this equality in liberty tends to fracture the natural order of hierarchy into an aggregate multitude since "in the framers' creed, [men] are by nature free, morally independent, [and] without obligations to nature or their fellows."[70]

By the early nineteenth century, the remnants of the hierarchical worldview tend to be swept away with the rising tide of Romanticism.[71] Historian Merle Curti explains the nature of this change: "The doctrine of a fixed order, with the elect irrevocably on one level and everyone else on another, hardly fitted the temper of a society in which individual initiative, industry, skill, and drive paid off."[72] But this new egalitarianism goes beyond rejecting the hereditary hierarchies of Europe; in this era, economic and social change, coupled with the onset of Jacksonian democracy, elicit a fresh view of human nature itself. Americans overturn the Great Chain of Being for the "belief in the emancipation of everyone…from the fixed authority of traditions and institutional restrictions."[73] Tocqueville marks the fundamental importance of this equality when defining the new American character: "the principal passion that agitates men…is the love of this equality."[74] Hierarchy of every sort—even intellectual superiority[75]—is impugned. Again, the result is the deposition of authority in favor of a chaotic democracy of opinion:

> Equality, which renders men independent of each other, makes them contract the habit and the taste of following their will alone in their particular actions. This entire independence, which they enjoy continually vis-à-vis their equals and in the practice of private life, disposes them to consider all authority with the eye of a malcontent and soon suggests to them the idea and love of political freedom….Of all the political effects that equality of conditions produces, it is this love of independence that first strikes one's regard and which most frightens timid spirits.[76]

The main obstacles to this equality were now to be the traditional hierarchical orders in religion and civic authority that "stymied democratic equality"[77] and which were now targeted to be eliminated. Whitman's multitude is now clamoring for recognition.

Indeed, the flattening effects of equality soon work their way into Americans' perception of religion. Since the Founders were equal parts English traditionalists, non-conformist Puritans, Enlightenment Deists, and a patchwork of other faiths (including atheists), the only practical solution in ordering society is to accept some form of pluralism. Gertrude Himmelfarb argues that political liberty could be assured only on condition that all religious positions were seen to be essentially equal.[78] But this implicitly requires religion to be less important than it had been. In the tradition of natural law, religion is seen to be the highest truth, the non-negotiable foundation for natural law. Now, it is relegated to private opinion, and so can be a foundation for nothing beyond personal conscience. This change is noticeable in the Founding documents themselves: while religion is central to the Declaration of Independence (as in Jefferson's reference to "Nature's God"), it is absent from the Constitution apart from its negative rule prohibiting religious tests.[79] A religion deprived of hierarchical eminence becomes a merely voluntaristic choice reflecting each individual's predilections.[80] It is interesting to note that in this way the doctrine of equality bears similar consequences for both church and state in the New World: both are subject to individual choice and so must be subordinate to the individual's aims. Just as equal atoms form a state and determine its laws, so individuals form churches and determine doctrine. As Perry recognizes, this voluntarist view of social order radically alters the meaning of obedience: "The contract theory in both of its forms implied that obedience is based upon a *quid pro quo*. It commended itself to the individual's reason because he, *qua* individual, could translate it into terms of his own consequent happiness or salvation."[81] In this circumstance, both tables of the Decalogue must be subject to revision, for instead of just relations predicated on obedience to a hierarchical order, now individuals are empowered to seek whatever enhances personal satisfaction.

The upending of traditional authority in favor of individuality and equality is made complete in the transcendentalism of Ralph Waldo Emerson. He proclaims that a "sign of our times, also marked by an analogous political movement, is the new importance given to the single person."[82] The basis for Emerson's newfound respect for individuality lies in his belief that God is manifest to all people as the spiritual animation present in Nature, and so can be intuited by everyone in terms of each individual's unique genius. As Emerson explains, "Nature is the opposite of the soul, answering to it part for part. One is seal, and one is print."[83] Because each man has within himself all truth, the very idea of hierarchy and authority become otiose. On the contrary, since each person is an authority unto himself, each must be true to himself; as Emerson advises, "To believe your own thought, to believe that what is true for you in your private heart is true for all men—that is genius."[84] Emerson sees that in rejecting hierarchy and authority, equality necessarily ushers in a radical autonomy: "No law can be sacred to me but that of my nature. Good and bad are but names very readily transferable to that or this; the only right is what is after my constitution, the only wrong what is against it."[85] If Emerson is correct, there is no place for natural law at all, and so obedience to it would be unthinkable.

Emerson's contemporary Theodore Parker[86] argued that Emerson embodies the new American notion of personal autonomy based on equality: "The results of human experience…the state, the church, society, the family, business, literature, science, art—all of these are subordinate to man; if they serve the individual, he is to foster them, if not, to abandon them and seek better things."[87] Authenticity to oneself replaces obedience to authority as the criterion for moral integrity. Each individual is the sole standard for his own excellence, so authority and hierarchy are dismissed as inherently oppressive.[88] W.K. Clifford nicely epitomizes the moral hazards of this atomistic equality: "There is one thing in the world more wicked than the desire to command and that is the will to obey."[89] Whitman's multitude is now is full flower.

The Critique of the American Creed of Equality

These facts drawn from American history seem to show clearly a movement away from hierarchical order to a populist egalitarianism. Further, that egalitarianism insensibly replaces the natural law in the self-understanding of the new nation.[90] To illustrate this more fully, I will invoke the analysis of a particularly acute observer of modern America, the journalist and public intellectual Walter Lippmann (1889-1974). His book from 1955, *The Public Philosophy*,[91] examines how deference to democratic processes led to the disasters of the twentieth century because of its implicit rejection of the natural law's demand to respect the authority of hierarchical powers.

The most fundamental consequence of the doctrine of equality, against the respect for hierarchical authority, is the assumption that every person's opinion carries equal significance. In democratic systems, this can become pathological when the people who exercise sovereign power do so in a way that makes it impossible for true authority to exercise prudential judgment in governance. Lippmann, surveying the first half of the twentieth century, supplies this diagnosis: "Where mass opinion dominates the government, there is a morbid derangement of the true functions of power. The derangement brings about the enfeeblement, verging on paralysis, of the capacity to govern. This...[is the] catastrophic decline of Western society."[92] While the Founders were self-confident in their ability to lead and did not "truckle to the people,"[93] in more recent decades this natural order has been inverted and "the people have imposed a veto upon the judgments of informed and responsible officials."[94] To get at the source of this deformation of democracy, Lippmann introduces a distinction between "The People" understood merely as the utilitarian sum of desires among the public, and "*The People*" as the collective wisdom of tradition ordered to the common good uniting the community's history with the interests of future generations yet unborn.[95] (Let us point out that the former is the Whitmanesque multitude, while the latter is the ordered hierarchy built on natural law.) Whenever the democratic impulse rejects the wisdom of the latter, it devolves to the former, becoming a Jacobin mob seeking to impose its general will on a nation.[96] It is this Jacobin apotheosis of the equality of opinion that has dominated American consciousness since the Romantic era and the rise of Jacksonian democracy.[97] This marks the repudiation of traditional natural law and the rise of a wholly modern liberalism that, while promising maximal liberty for the individual, can never fulfill that promise because of its erosion of a social order based on authority.

For Lippmann, the real problem with this Jacobin gospel of equality is that it actively discourages the pursuit of perfection, the attainment of virtue by which one man really distinguishes himself from the mob. As he puts it,

> Relying on the inherent rightness of the natural impulses of man's first nature, the Jacobin theory does away with the second civilized nature, with the ruler of the impulses, which is identified with the grand necessities of the commonwealth. It overthrows the ruler within each man,—he who exercises "the royal and political rule" over his "irascible and concupiscible powers." When reason no longer represents society within the human psyche, then it becomes the instrument of appetite, desire, and passion.[98]

It is because man refuses to accept a well-ordered hierarchy that he cannot be free to discover perfection. Rather, he is enslaved to desires, a Hobbesian state in which conflict with others is inevitable. It is not by accident that Whitman's multitude was first celebrated in a poem called "Song of Myself,"[99] for denying the authority of reason also isolates the individual to the subjectivity of his passions which, in turn, makes social harmony impossible.

Lippmann sees that in this way, the attack on public authority—the insistence that there is no qualitative distinction between opinions—corresponds with the erosion of the authority of reason within man. If no thing is superior to any other, every impulse is self-justifying. This is also a repudiation of the wisdom of the past, for tradition has no authority over contemporary taste. Modern democratic societies, then, are unmoored from the sources on which their successful societies were built.[100] Lacking objective criteria for moral choice and principles for making public policy decisions, the state is governed by the capricious demands of the mob. Democracy, which had promised a stable and orderly pursuit of the common good, becomes the instrument of ephemeral passions and utopian dreams.[101]

As Daniel Mahoney has recently observed, "Fanatical egalitarianism is an invitation to unabashed tyranny....Radical egalitarianism wars with the highest in human beings and thus mutilates man....[It] reveals the destructive face of utopia cut off from God and a natural order of things. It is anti-human in decisive respects."[102]

When equality is defined in opposition to hierarchy, religion suffers, morality is degraded, and democracy degenerates into mob rule. These depredations can only be avoided by returning to the natural law and accepting the hierarchy by which order is restored.

Conclusion: The Normative Necessity of Hierarchy

Francis Slade has argued that essential to the natural law is the capacity to distinguish one's personal aims from mankind's objective ends.[103] This distinction itself assumes the recognition of hierarchy, since it requires that a person subject his desires to a critique from the authority of reason and social superiors (not to mention divine revelation). Indeed, the more one defers to authority—whether divine or human—the more objectified and communal desires become, and the better ordered society will be to attain the common good. On the other hand, the less one defers to authority, the more subjective preference is indulged and the more chaotic society becomes, since in pursuing personal interests society is atomized. It is for good reason that the most important precepts of the natural law indicate the need to subordinate oneself to God and temporal authority.

Americans now live by the creed of equality, which teaches that the there is no authority over the individual. This is immediately evident in the decline of the virtue of piety in contemporary culture. Thomas defines piety as a debt owed to those who are responsible for the being and governance of others.[104] It is, in fact, nothing other than the obediential deference to hierarchy given by those who benefit from another's authority. As Augustine argued, the most fundamental good of any society is this tranquility of order,[105] the peace without which human flourishing in impossible. Natural law acknowledges this in commanding piety and gratitude from all citizens whose common good depends on this peaceful order. The multitude, in rejecting authority, also contemns both gratitude and piety. The doctrine of equality thus subverts all the hierarchies on which the natural law is built. Let us consider these in order, starting with law and proceeding through society to human nature and finally God Himself.

First, the assumption of equality casts the First and Fourth commandments into a very different light. With equality, there is no ascertainable common good apart from individual desires. Therefore, the demand to defer to authority for the common good becomes inherently irrational. The only way to salvage the law is to view it in terms of mere voluntaristic dictates by which some are subject to the arbitrary will of others. The law becomes an act of power, not authority, with no intrinsic relation to goodness.

The polis, too, must suffer. If there is no natural basis for establishing authoritative governance, then the only criterion for legitimacy is consent of the people. But this consent is an arbitrary and ephemeral act of will; it is subject to the blandishments of the ambitious, who challenge one another in a race to the bottom. This lowest-common-denominator version of democracy, far from securing peace and the common good, is guaranteed only to bring constant strife as rights are continually discovered to arouse the appetite of the insatiable public.

This political problem is grounded in the deeper problem of rejecting the authority of reason over other psychic faculties. If there is no natural hierarchy in the soul, then the judgments of reason are no more obliging than the yearnings of passion and appetite. As a result, no activity can be called normative for man; any act may be justified as "authentically" human simply because a man does it. Man disintegrates into conflicting impulses which, in the absence of authoritative order, can no longer attain peace.

Finally, since there is no evidence of hierarchy anywhere in nature, the analogical hierarchy ordering creature to Creator becomes increasingly untenable. Man, then, is in constant rebellion against the order of the cosmos itself. This is evidenced in the spiritual crises that Deneen sees as proof of the failure of liberalism. The rejection of a hierarchical ordering of man to God deprives him of finding a transcendent meaning in life, and so human existence becomes pointless.

This universe of equality, instead of fulfilling man's most profound dreams, in the end evacuates life of significance. To hold all opinions as equal, to claim that there is nothing more noble than anything else, is to eliminate any reason for acting at all. If actions neither perfect nor harm, there is nothing to motivate, and no criterion by which to evaluate. There is no basis for order at all, and so we are left, like Whitman, celebrating diversity for its own sake. Nothing is honorable and nothing is contemptible, and so we revel in incoherent contradictions.

If this is the fruit of the doctrine of equality, we can only ask now whether our nation, or any nation so conceived and so dedicated, can long endure.

Notes

1. Patrick J. Deneen, *Why Liberalism Failed* (New Haven: Yale University Press, 2018), 21-42. See the review in this volume.
2. John Courtney Murray, S.J., *We Hold These Truths* (New York: Sheed and Ward, 1960), 27-43. Murray was not alone in this estimation, for roughly at the same time Jacques Maritain made similar observations in *Reflections on America* (New York: Charles Scribner's Sons, 1958), 193-200.
3. Robert Reilly, "For God and Country: Can Good Christians be Good Americans," *The Claremont Review of Books* XVII.3 (Summer 2017), 44-50. Reilly is reviewing Deneen's earlier book, *Conserving America?: Essays on Present Discontents* (South Bend, IN: St. Augustine's Press, 2016), in addition to works by Rod Dreher and Michael Hanby. The debate continued with a number of essays from both Reilly and Deneen, as well as other commentators, at *The Public Discourse* blog in September and October 2017.
4. This is simply to acknowledge the pluralistic nature of the American founding. Indeed, the historians cited later in this paper encounter the same issue, for whenever they want to make a generalization about the Founding era, they have to simultaneously recognize the many counter-examples to be found representing the opposite position.
5. *Summa Theologiae* I-II.91.2, slightly paraphrasing two separate definitions: "this participation of the eternal law in the rational creature is called the natural law" and "the natural law is nothing else than the rational creature's participation of the eternal law." *Summa Theologica*, trans. Fathers of the English Dominican Province (1948; reprint, Allen, TX: Christian Classics, 1981).
6. Ibid., I-II.91.1.
7. Ibid., I.44.proem; cf. *Summa Contra Gentiles*, III.97.11: "Therefore, just as the first rational principle of divine providence is simply the divine goodness, so the first rational principle in creatures is their numerical plurality, to the establishment and conservation of which all other things seem to be ordered." *Summa Contra Gentiles*, trans. Anton C. Pegis, James F. Anderson, Vernon J. Bourke, and Charles J. O'Neil (1955; reprint, Notre Dame, IN: Notre Dame University Press, 1975).
8. *Summa Theologiae*, I.20.3.
9. Ibid., I.19.2-3 and I.44.4.
10. Ibid., I.6.1-4.
11. Ibid., I.47.1.
12. *Summa Contra Gentiles*, I.43.8; cf. *De ente et essentia*, c. 4.
13. *Summa Theologiae*, I.44.1.
14. Ibid., I.47.2.
15. *Summa Contra Gentiles*, III.97.4: "Now, from the diversity of forms by which the species of things are differentiated there also results a difference of operations. For, since everything acts in so far as it is actual (because things that are potential are found by that very fact to be devoid of action), and since every being is actual through form, it is necessary for the operation of a thing to follow its form. Therefore, if there are different forms, they must have different operations." Cf. *Summa Contra Gentiles*, II.68.7.
16. *Summa Theologiae*, I.105.5.
17. *Summa Contra Gentiles*, II.45.4.
18. *Summa Theologiae*, I-II.93.1: "The eternal law is nothing else than the type of Divine Wisdom, as directing all actions and movements."

19. Ibid., I.22.4.
20. Ibid., 103.6; cf. DV 5.8. In *Summa Contra Gentiles*, III.69.16-17, Thomas argues that all creatures act together for the sake of a common good, the perfection of the universe.
21. *Summa Contra Gentiles*, III.81. We should note that there are two important exceptions to this principle that difference implies hierarchy: the persons of the Trinity (*Summa Theologiae*, I.39.1-2), and the complementary nature of man and woman, especially as realized in marriage (*Summa Theologiae*, I.92.1 and 3).
22. See W. Norris Clarke, S.J., *The One and the Many: A Contemporary Thomistic Metaphysics* (Notre Dame, IN:University of Notre Dame Press, 2001), 306.
23. Thomas is here simply following the inherited insights of Plato, esp. in *Republic* IV, where justice is to "rule and be ruled according to nature" (447d7), so that reason rules the appetites and emotions.
24. *Commentary on the "Book of Causes,"* Propositions 18-19, tr. by Vincent A. Guagliardo, O.P., Charles O. Hess, O.P., and Richard C. Taylor (Washington: The Catholic University of America Press, 1996).
25. *De Veritate*, 2.2: "[The highest perfection of a creature] consists in this, that the perfection belonging to one thing is found in another. This is the perfection of a knower in so far as he knows....In this way it is possible for the perfection of the entire universe to exist in one thing. The ultimate perfection which the soul can attain, therefore, is, according to the philosophers, to have delineated in it the entire order and causes of the universe. This they held to be the ultimate end of man." From *Truth*, trans. Robert W. Mulligan, S.J., James V. McGlynn, S.J., and Robert W. Schmidt, S.J. (Chicago: Henry Regnery, 1954).
26. *Summa Theologiae*, I.76.1 and 3.
27. Ibid., I.81.3.ad 2.
28. Ibid., I-II.19.3.
29. Ibid., I-II.18.1-2.
30. Ibid., I-II.71.2 and ad 3.
31. Ibid., I-II.19.4 and I-II.21.1.
32. *De Regminine* I.13. This echoes Augustine in *City of God*, XIX.17, who says since the life of a city—both of Man and of God—are social, we need to obey the ruler in each in order to attain harmonious peace.
33. *De Regimine* I.1; translation from *Aquinas: Political Writings* edited and translated by in R.W. Dyson (Cambridge: Cambridge University Press, 2002).
34. *Commentary on Aristotle's Politics*, I.1.7.
35. *Summa Contra Gentiles*, III.81.5.
36. *Summa Theologiae*, I-II.93.3 and 95.2.
37. Ibid., I.96.3-4.
38. Ibid., I.96.3.ad 3.
39. Ibid., II-II.104.1; in the second reply, he explicitly compares obedience to a human authority to obedience to God's will.
40. See Ibid., I.90.2 for creation of the soul; also *Summa Contra Gentiles*, II.80-81.7-8 for commensuration with body, and II.68.3 for the unity of form and matter in a single act of existence.
41. *Summa Contra Gentiles*, III.97.4-9.
42. *Summa Theologiae*, I-II.91.2.

43. Ibid., II-II.58.1.
44. Ibid., I-II.94.2.
45. *Summa Contra Gentiles*, III.112.5: "Each intellectual substance is, in a way, all things. For it may comprehend the entirety of being through its intellect"; and *Summa Theologiae*, I-II.3.8: "Consequently, when man knows an effect, and knows that it has a cause, there naturally remains in the man the desire to know about the cause, 'what it is.'"
46. *Summa Theologiae*, I.108.6. and 3: "Love as the lover is united to the object loved....Therefore to know lower things is better than to love them; and to love the higher things, God above all, is better than to know them."
47. Ibid., I.16.5 and I.6.2.
48. Ibid., I-II.100.1, 3, and 11.
49. Ibid., II-II.122.2; cf. *Collationes de Decem Praeceptis*, 3.
50. Ibid., II-II.122.5: "The precepts of the decalogue are directed to the love of God and of our neighbor. Now to our parents, of all our neighbors, we are under the greatest obligation. Hence, immediately after the precepts directing us to God, a place is given to the precept directing us to our parents, who are the particular principle of our being, just as God is the universal principle." Cf. *Collationes de Decem Praeceptis*, 6.
51. Ibid., II-II.101.1: "Man becomes a debtor to other men in various ways, according to their various excellences and the various benefits received from them. On both counts God holds first place, for He is supremely excellent, and is for us the first principle of being and government. On the second place, the principles of our being and government are our parents and our country, that have given us birth and nourishment. Consequently man is debtor chiefly to his parents and his country, after God. Wherefore just as it belongs to religion to give worship to God, so does it belong to piety, in the second place, to give worship to one's parents and one's country."
52. I follow the argument of Yves Simon, *A General Theory of Authority* (Notre Dame, IN: University of Notre Dame Press, 1962), 137-39.
53. Simon, *A General Theory of Authority*, 154. It is important to distinguish this hierarchical authority from a mere exercise of power. As Heinrich Rommen points out in *The State in Catholic Thought: A Treatise in Political Philosophy* (St. Louis and London: B. Herder Book Co., 1945), 380-83, power is the ability to effect one's will; however, because humans are free rational beings, obedience to power is never blind. Immediately upon recognizing the ontological superiority of God, people willingly obey Him. But people will only obey human edict as authoritative so long as it embodies the moral authority of acting for the good of all as determined by the rule of reason—the natural law. Thus, power must be subject to the natural law to take on the cloak of authority, or else it becomes a despotic assertion of will.
54. *Commentary on the Nicomachean Ethics*, VIII.7.1632.
55. John Rawls, *Political Liberalism* (New York: Columbia University Press, 1993), 3-7.
56. Indeed, John Courtney Murray (*We Hold These Truths*, 298-99) recognizes the blunder of even calling this new thought *natural law*: "The nineteenth centu-

ry exhibited those extensive powers of learned misunderstanding which it possessed to an astonishing degree. In its extraordinary ignorance of philosophical and legal history, it supposed that the 'law of nature' of the Age of the Enlightenment was the *ius naturale*, of an earlier and in many ways more enlightened age."

57. Walt Whitman, *Leaves of Grass*, Book III: "Song of Myself", section 51, lines 6-8. It might be argued that Whitman is speaking of himself here, as the title clearly would imply. But I believe he is employing a sort of synecdoche in which he represents the American multitude within himself.
58. Ralph Barton Perry, *Puritanism and Democracy* (New York: Vanguard Press, 1944), 163-67.
59. Locke, *Second Treatise of Government*, II.6: "The state of Nature has a law of Nature to govern it, which obliges every one, and reason, which is that law, teaches all mankind who will but consult it, that being all equal and independent, no one ought to harm another in his life, health, liberty or possessions… so by the like reason, when his own preservation comes not in competition, ought he as much as he can to preserve the rest of mankind."
60. Murray, *We Hold These Truths*, 303; the citation is from Locke's *Second Treatise*, IX.123.
61. Perry, *Puritanism and Democracy*, 164.
62. Luis Cortest, *The Disfigured Face: Traditional Natural Law and Its Encounter with Modernity* (New York: Fordham University Press, 2008), 53.
63. On this shift from duties to rights, see Henry Veatch, "Natural Law: Dead or Alive?" in *Literature of Liberty: A Review of Contemporary Liberal Thought* vol. 1, no. 4 (Oct.-Dec. 1978), 7-31, especially 16-18.
64. Perry, *Puritanism and Democracy*, 417.
65. Perry, *Puritanism and Democracy*, 556. John Courtney Murray finds three sources for the errors of Locke's version of natural law: its rationalism, individualism, and nominalism (*We Hold These Truths*, 305). The last of these is the ultimate foundation for the problem, since if each thing is radically and simply unique, there is then no basis for an analogical hierarchy of being. My argument assumes the problematic nature of this metaphysical position.
66. David Wootton, *Power, Pleasure, and Profit: Insatiable Appetites from Machiavelli to Madison* (Cambridge, MA: The Belknap Press of Harvard University Press, 2018), 15.
67. Wootton, *Power*, 71.
68. Thomas G. West, *The Political Theory of the American Founding: Natural Rights, Public Policy, and the Moral Conditions of Freedom* (Cambridge: Cambridge University Press, 2017), 21.
69. This statement is from Wilson Carey McWilliams, cited in West, *Political Theory*, 28.
70. West, *Political Theory*, 36.
71. Merle Curti, *Human Nature in American Thought: A History* (Madison: University of Wisconsin Press, 1980), 43-69. It should be noted that the idea of hierarchy in nature remained part of the American debate through the writings of the Federalists (see *Federalist 10's* discussion of factions arising from unequal talent), and especially John Adams (see Curti, *Human Nature*, 106-46). Thus, Whitman's multitude included those who defend the tradition, though they are effectively drowned out by other voices.

72. Curti, *Human Nature*, 79.
73. Curti, *Human Nature*, 103.
74. Alexis de Tocqueville, *Democracy in America*, tr. by Harvey C. Mansfield and Delba Winthrop (Chicago: University of Chicago Press, 2000): II.2.1, 480.
75. Ibid., II.3.21, 613.
76. Ibid., II.4.1, 639. This sense of equality against authority takes on a metaphysical character in the notion that all men are equal in being infinitely perfectible (Tocqueville, *Democracy in America*, II.1.8, 426-28). As founding father Benjamin Rush averred in 1786, "I am as full persuaded, that from the combined action of causes…it is possible to produce such a change in [man's] moral character, as shall raise him to a resemblance of angels—nay more, to the likeness of God Himself" (cited in Curti, *Human Nature*, 70).
77. Curti, *Human Nature*, 93.
78. Gertrude Himmelfarb, *The Roads to Modernity: The British, French, and American Enlightenments* (New York: Alfred A. Knopf, 2005), 191.
79. Himmelfarb, *Roads to Modernity*, 204.
80. Murray, *We Hold These Truths*, 276-89.
81. Perry, *Puritanism and Democracy*, 194. In fact, Thomas Paine, the most radical of the Founders, locates the source of equality in the Bible itself: "The Mosaic account of the creation, whether taken as divine authority or merely historical, is full to this point [of] the unity or equality of man. The expressions admits of no controversy. 'And God said, Let us make man in our own image. In the image of God created he him; male and female created he them.' The distinction of sexes is pointed out, but no other distinction is even implied. If this be not divine authority, it is at least historical authority, and shows that the equality of man, so far from being a modern doctrine, is the oldest upon record." See Paine, *The Rights of Man*, (Harmondsworth and New York: Penguin Books, 1984), 66-67.
82. Ralph Waldo Emerson, "The American Scholar," in John J. Stuhr, ed., *Pragmatism and Classical American Philosophy*, second edition, (Oxford: Oxford University Press, 2000), 26.
83. Emerson, "The American Scholar," 18. See also this comment from "Self-Reliance": "The relations of the soul to the divine spirit are so pure, that it is profane to seek to interpose helps" (in Stuhr, 33).
84. Emerson, "Self-Reliance," in Stuhr, 27.
85. Emerson, "Self-Reliance," 28.
86. Parker (1810-1860) was an influential Unitarian pastor who is the source for Martin Luther King's famous adage about the arc of the moral universe bending toward justice.
87. Cited in Curti, *Human Nature*, 184.
88. Although he does not name Emerson, this is Charles Taylor's critique of post-modernity's remaking of identity in *The Ethics of Authenticity* (Cambridge, MA: Harvard University Press, 1991), 66.
89. Cited in Simon, *A General Theory of Authority*, 148.
90. Indeed, Murray's critique of modern versions of natural law is entitled "The Doctrine is Dead," but this is followed by a chapter, "The Doctrine Lives," proclaiming the "eternal return" of true natural law.
91. Walter Lippmann, *The Public Philosophy* (New Brunswick and London: Transaction Publishers, 2010).

92. Ibid., 15.
93. Ibid., 26.
94. Ibid., 20.
95. Ibid., 38: "While *The People* as a corporate body are the true owners of the sovereign power, The People, as an aggregate of voters, have diverse, conflicting, self-centered interests and opinions. A plurality of them cannot be counted upon to represent the corporate nation." Lippmann comments that as The People grows and diversifies, its public opinion necessarily becomes less realistic.
96. The *Federalist* saw the Constitution as a bulwark and factionalism of any sort as being rule by a mob; as Madison notes in *Federalist* 55: "In all very numerous assemblies, of whatever character composed, passion never fails to wrest the sceptre from reason. Had every Athenian citizen been a Socrates, every Athenian assembly would still have been a mob."
97. Lippmann, 66. Yves Simon concurs on the deleterious impact of Jackson; see *Philosophy of Democratic Government* (Chicago: University of Chicago Press, 1951): 144-54. John Courtney Murray recognized that it was precisely the American Revolution's acceptance of God and the authority of natural law that distinguished it from the French Revolution: "[T]he sovereignty of God over nations as well as over individual men…is the principle that radically distinguishes the conservative Christian tradition of America from the Jacobin laicist tradition of Continental Europe….Part of the inner architecture of the American ideal of freedom has been the profound conviction that only a virtuous people can be free. It is not an American belief that free government is inevitable, only that it is possible, and that its possibility can be realized only when the people as a whole are inwardly governed by the recognized imperatives of the universal moral law." See *We Hold These Truths*, 28 and 36.
98. Lippmann, 77; cf. 162.
99. The Emersonian influence is evident in the opening section of the poem: "I celebrate myself, and sing myself, / And what I assume you shall assume, / For every atom belonging to me as good belongs to you…. // Creeds and schools in abeyance, / Retiring back a while sufficed at what they are, but never forgotten, / I harbor for good or bad, I permit to speak at every hazard, / Nature without check with original energy."
100. Lippmann, 96: This "is the central and critical condition of the Western society: that the democracies are ceasing to receive the traditions of civility in which the good society, the liberal, democratic way of life at its best, originated and developed. They are cut off from the public philosophy….They are proletarians who are 'in' but are not 'of' the society they dominate."
101. Lippmann, 142: "The radical error of the modern democratic gospel is that it promises, not the good life of this world, but the perfect life of heaven."
102. Daniel J. Mahoney, *The Idol of Our Age: How the Religion of Humanity Subverts Christianity* (New York: Encounter Books, 2018), 3.
103. Francis Slade, "Ends and Purposes" in Richard F. Hassing, ed., *Final Causality in Nature and Human Affairs* (Washington, DC: The Catholic University of America Press, 1997), 83-85.
104. *Summa Theologiae*, II-II.101.3.
105. Augustine, *City of God*, XIX.13.

Participation and the Thomistic Definition of Natural Law

Catherine Peters

In both Thomas Aquinas's treatise on law (*Summa Theologiae*, I-II, qq. 90-108) and the tradition following him, natural law is closely allied with metaphysics, such that whenever metaphysics is dismissed the richness of natural law tends to be overlooked as well. A metaphysical element of central importance to his legal treatise is "participation," as is evident in the traditionally accepted definition of natural law as "nothing else than a participation of the eternal law in a rational creature."[1] But while debates concerning the natural law in general and Thomistic natural law in particular abound, the precise meaning of participation is often left largely unexplored.[2] This neglect has occurred despite a general increase of interest in this topic following the revival of Thomistic scholarship in the twentieth century.[3] The present study seeks to remedy this oversight by presenting the meaning and modes of participation and its employment within Thomas's definition of natural law. In so doing, it will show the importance of recognizing natural law as a kind of participation in order to meet the general requirements for law as "a certain ordinance of reason, to the common good, from him who has care of the community, and promulgated."[4]

Thomas Aquinas on the Meaning and Modes of Participation

Etymologically, "participation" means to take a part of something and is, indeed, sometimes simply defined by Thomas as being "nothing else than to take partially from another."[5] W. Norris Clarke identifies three elements indicative of participation: first, the source of the participated perfections possesses it in a total manner. Second, the participating being possesses the same perfection but in a limited way. Third, the participating being depends in some way on the source of the perfection.[6] While these requirements can certainly be gleaned from the Thomistic corpus, Thomas's own most extensive and technical treatment of this topic is found within a commentary on the *De ebdomadibus* of Boethius. In this work, Thomas begins with a general description of participation as a kind of taking part, but then immediately delineates three specific modes in which this can occur.[7]

The first is of a species in a genus or an individual in a species; the second is of a subject in an accident or matter in form; the third is of an effect in a cause. Common to each mode is limitation of the thing taking part, and participation thus implies finitude on the part of the participator. A species, subject or matter, and effect take part in but do not exhaust the genus, accident or form, and cause. Within this commentary, Thomas focuses on the third mode to account for the participation of creatures in existence and goodness. This mode is also the clearest employment of "participation" within the definition of natural law. But this is not to say that the first two modes are unimportant when trying to understand Thomas's account of natural law. It is my contention that "participation" in the first mode supplies a framework for seeing the traditional definition as supplying a kind of genus and species of natural law. The second mode can be seen in a natural being, namely the rational creature, participating in the eternal law itself, akin to a subject taking part in an accident or matter being informed. The third mode shows the causal relation between natural and eternal law and explicates the way in which we come to an understanding of the eternal law from the natural. In this way, each of the modes of participation can shed light on Thomas's presentation of natural law and its relation to the eternal law.

Before exploring these specific applications, however, one should note that Thomas insists that participation is properly descriptive of creatures' relation to God, and thus the commonality between the participators and what they are participating in cannot be univocal nor, at the same time, can God be said to participate in anything. While participation is indicative of the relation between God and creatures, this does not warrant any univocal predication between them. As Thomas explains,

> there is nothing said about God through participation: for everything that participates is determined to the mode of the

> participant, and thus it has it partially and not according to the mode of perfection. It is necessary, then, that nothing is predicated univocally of God and of creatures.[8]

One can discern here—especially in the third mode of participation—the reasoning later employed to account for how we can name or attribute things to God through analogy (as presented, for example, in *Summa Theologiae*, I, qq. 12-13) because, as Thomas explains elsewhere, "all things from God, insofar as they are beings, are like the first and universal principle of all existence."[9]

To summarize, "participation" as a kind of "taking part" is manifested in three modes: something particular in something more universal (species in genus or individual in species), matter in form or substance in accident, and effect in cause. In each of these modes, the participant takes part but does not exhaust that in which it is participating. When applied to the relation between God and creatures, the participation is on the side of creatures, and thus even the perfections in which they take part can only be analogously attributed to God. Having given a cursory presentation of these modes, it is now possible to see more clearly the meaning of each mode within its particular application to natural law.

Natural Law and the First Mode of Participation

The first mode of participation in which "something receives in a particular way that which pertains to another universally" is when a species partakes in a genus or an individual partakes in its species.[10] The species or individual is part of the genus or species, but in a limited way. For this reason, "man is said to participate in animal, because he does not have the *ratio* of animal according to its total commonality" and this schema can be applied to individuals because "by the same reason Socrates participates in man."[11] The species participates insofar as it shares in but does not encompass the genus (and, in this same way, the individual takes part in the species).

For present purposes, the first mode is of particular value in demonstrating that Thomas's definition conveys how the natural law is a genuine law by identifying it as a species falling under the genus of "taking part in the eternal law," that to which all laws must ultimately be traced.[12] Now, at this point one should distinguish "participation in eternal law" taken as a genus from the eternal law itself. The eternal law itself cannot be a proper genus because it is ultimately identified with God, and thus it is beyond all genera taken in a strict sense.[13] The first mode of participation, however, can establish "participation in eternal law" as a genus insofar as each of the specific kinds of law are traced back to the eternal law in a relation akin to that of a genus and species. Indeed, Thomas even goes so far as to say that if a law were to deviate from this partaking it would no longer have the nature of law "but of violence."[14] Any semblance to true law that such a perversion might possess is allowed only because it has been promulgated, and such an act of authority is at least reminiscent of the legislative power of the eternal law. But this resemblance is not sufficient to render it a law, and for this reason Thomas ends his reply by quoting Augustine's claim that "in temporal law there is nothing just and lawful but what man has drawn from the eternal law."[15] All true laws, then, must fall under the eternal law, and the first mode of participation explains how this is brought about.

Thomas's own example is of "man" participating in "animal" to establish the definition of man as "rational animal" through this first mode of participation. The genus here is "animal" while the specific difference is "rational." The species participates in the genus but does not exhaust it, because there are certainly animals that do not possess this specific difference. Omitting either part of this definition would lead to a defective understanding of man. Similarly, to have a full definition of natural law must include reference to the genus by which it is a law and to the difference that makes it to be a specific kind. This kind of participatory relation can be seen in Thomas's definition of natural law as a participation in the eternal law, a formal definition conveying the essence of natural law. In sum, "participation in eternal law" can stand as a genus and natural law is a species differentiated by the nature of human participation in it. Just as "rational" participates in "animal" such that we have a definition of man, similarly it is natural law's relation to eternal law that makes it to be fully a law while it is specified by the difference of nature or human rationality, as Thomas puts it, "in the rational creature." The connection of natural law to eternal law is indispensable for Thomas who, indeed, even goes so far as to explicitly say that the natural law is not diverse from the eternal law, though it is present in the creature in a finite way.[16] In so doing, Thomas recognizes the particular kind of participation that the rational creature is capable of is always according to its own imperfect mode.[17]

Some, such as Martin Rhonheimer, are concerned that the traditional definition's inclusion of eternal law runs the risk of "a truncated conception" of natural law that ignores how it is "in the rational creature" and instead promotes as a definition another passage from Thomas's account of natural law that it is "nothing other than the light of understanding infused in us by God, whereby we understand what must be done and what must be avoided."[18] The formal definition of natural law, Rhonheimer thus maintains, is not the final sentence of Thomas's reply but the preceding one.[19] But just as man is not the cause of his own being, so too the natural law is not the cause of its own legality.[20] To define natural law solely in terms of *human* reason ignores this point and thereby fails as a sufficient definition. The traditional definition does not disregard the human element but rather emphasizes that natural law is a genuine *law* because of its relation to the eternal law, in which the rational creature takes part, and not because of its human source. Rhonheimer's own preferred definition, it should be noted, is susceptible to the same critiques he raises to the traditional definition.[21] In sum, employing the first mode of participation establishes a framework for understanding what the natural law essentially is: participation in the eternal law (genus) in the rational creature (species).

Natural Law and the Second Mode of Participation

Participation occurs in a second mode when "a subject participates in an accident, and matter in form, because substantial or accidental form, which is common by its own *ratio*, is determined to this or that subject…"[22] Thomas treats both of these examples (subject in accident, matter in form) as the same kind of participation because, as Stephen Brock explains, both reference the commonality of form. What receives a form, accidental or substantial, constrains it to this particular instance, whether the participator be an already constituted subject or prime matter itself.[23] Form is something common that, when contracted by a recipient, is made particular and limited. In this way, the subject or matter takes part in form.

While this mode is left largely unemployed within the *De ebdomadibus* commentary, it can nonetheless assist us in understanding the way in which natural subjects take part in the eternal law. Like a subject taking part in an accident, natural law as a participatory effect of eternal law can be seen as accidental to the participator. Now, one might immediately object that to characterize the natural law as an accident to the natural subject underplays the central importance of the natural law. But Thomas himself uses the relation between subject and accident to describe the relation between essence and existence, using "accident" in the non-specific sense of anything not included within the essence of the thing. Thus he says that "accident is said broadly of everything that is not part of the essence; and thus is existence in created things because in God alone is existence of His essence."[24] Similarly, the natural law as participation in eternal law is not the very essence of the natural participator and can be seen as standing in a kind of accidental relation to it. The eternal law is nonetheless present within the rational creature through the participation of natural law as a "rule and measure" which orders man to his proper acts and end.[25] This rational participation in the eternal law is effected according to the mode of the participator, which, Thomas reminds us, is always imperfect.[26]

All things are subject to the eternal law insofar as they participate in existence, but this participation is always relative to what kind of being is participating. Because law is essentially rational, the participation of non-rational beings is a similitude of natural law, made possible because participation in existence entails participation in providence to some extent and in some way. But this participation is only law in the full sense when performed by rational creatures because law is essentially a dictate of reason. As Thomas himself explains, human participation is "more excellent" than the partaking of non-rational beings because man is able to knowingly participate in divine providence:

> among other beings the rational creature is subject more excellently to the mode of divine providence insofar as it is a sharer in divine providence, providing for itself and others. And hence the eternal reason is participated in it, through which it has a natural inclination to its proper act and end. And such participation of the eternal law in the rational creature is called natural law.[27]

The participation of brute animals in eternal law, then, is merely a similitude of the natural law.[28] Emphasizing the importance of the eternal law in Thomas's account, then, does not diminish the role of human participation, because rational participation is constitutive of natural law.

Natural Law and the Third Mode of Participation

The third and final mode of participation is that of an effect in its cause. As Thomas explains, "an effect is said to participate in its cause, and especially when it is not equal to the power of its cause."[29] The example he gives is of air participating in the light of the sun, from which it receives illumination. Within the *De ebdomadibus* commentary this mode is employed to account for the existential participation of creatures in God and it is also of central importance when explicating the relation between the eternal and natural law. Not only is natural law the result of human participation in the eternal law—and in this way it is an effect of the eternal law—but it is also indispensable when seeking to answer the question of whether one needs prior and explicit knowledge of the eternal law in order to grasp the natural.

If Thomas held that one needed explicit knowledge of the eternal law (and hence God) in order to know the natural law, he would immediately encounter a difficulty. He maintains, on the one hand, that the existence of God is not self-evident.[30] Yet, on the other, he claims that the first precepts of natural law cannot but be known by all.[31] But how would it be possible for man to always know the natural law if it relies on a proposition that is *not* self-evident? Happily, Thomas does not hold this. As he explains, something can be known in two ways:

> One way, in itself. In the other way, in its effects, in which some kind of likeness of it is found. Just as one does not see the sun in its substance, but knows it in its radiance. Thus, therefore, it is said that the eternal law is not able to be known in itself except by the blessed, who see God through His essence. But every rational creature can know it in its radiance, either better or worse. For every knowledge of truth is a kind of radiance and participation of the eternal law, which is immutable truth.[32]

Natural law is a participation in eternal law and stands in relation to it in the same way that an effect is related to its cause.[33] It is this third mode of participation that allows one to defend the traditional definition from claims that the natural law thus defined is rendered somehow unintelligible apart from the eternal law.

Following the generally Aristotelian approach of beginning with what is more knowable to us before moving to what is more knowable in itself, Thomas presents our knowledge of the eternal law and of God as beginning with effects. Compare the following passage on knowledge of the existence of God with the one just quoted regarding knowledge of the eternal law:

> Something can be self-evident in two ways. One way, in itself but not to us. The other way, in itself and to us….The proposition that God exists, is self-evident in itself because the predicate is in the subject, for God is his own existence…. But because we do not know God as He is it is not self-evident to us, but requires demonstration through things that are more evident to us and less known in their nature, namely through effects.[34]

This passage shows a clear parallel between coming to knowledge of God through His effects and of the eternal law through natural law. Neither requires that we begin with explicit knowledge of a cause to know its effects. But, according to Thomas, "existence, which is in created things, is not able to be understood unless as derived from divine existence; just as a proper effect cannot be understood unless as derived from its proper cause."[35] The discovery of natural law—as traditionally defined—does not rest on a demonstration that moves from a cause to its effects, but rather follows a demonstration of effects to cause, the typical approach of Thomas in matters concerning creatures and the Creator.[36] Such methodology, far from rendering natural law dependent on explicit theological knowledge, is a thoroughly philosophical investigation that leads to but does not begin with theological claims.[37]

Referencing the eternal law does not, then, presuppose knowledge of it in order to understand the natural law.[38] This is nonetheless a charge Martin Rhonheimer has levied at a metaphor employed by Steven Long, which could seem at first to warrant such a reproach. As Long puts it, natural law without God is "like opera without voices: that is, it is a contradiction in terms that even were it possible still could command no normative attention."[39] Every analogy limps, of course, but this one can be salvaged when one recognizes it as referring not to the order of discovery but to the order of being. Understood in this way, natural law is impossible without God, the eternal law, because He is the cause of the natural law. Furthermore, natural law is explicitly identified by Thomas with the eternal law, and thus to deny the existence of the eternal law is ultimately to deny the existence of natural law. The order of being that Long's analogy corresponds to is the reverse of the order of discovery in which one moves from what is better known to us (natural law) to that which is better known in itself (the eternal law), and these orders must be distinguished.[40] Only then can the ontological priority of the eternal law to the natural law be understood while recognizing the epistemological priority of the natural law.[41]

Participation and the Legal Character of Natural Law

Each of the modes of participation outlined in the *De ebdomadibus* commentary can be seen within Thomas's definition and account of natural law. The first allows an identification of natural law as a specific kind of law, with "participation in eternal law" serving as a genus for the definition. The second mode illuminates how the natural subject takes part in the eternal law, in a relation akin to a subject taking part in an accident or matter being receptive of form, such that natural law is present as a kind of accident in the rational creature. The third mode, most importantly, accounts for the causal relation between God (the eternal law) and creatures (natural participators), which accounts not only for how the natural law is present in the creature (as explained through the second mode) but also how it is related to the eternal law (which allows an identification of a kind of genus and difference through the first mode). While the third is the most important mode within the context of natural law, each of them sheds light on Thomas's account. "Participation" is thus an indispensable interpretive key to understanding his definition of natural law, one deeply grounded in a metaphysical understanding of creatures' ontological dependence on God. But "participation" is also important for understanding how natural law is situated within Thomas's own treatise on law and, as law, can answer the legal requirements established in *Summa Theologiae*, I-II, a. 90.

There Thomas begins with a general definition of law as "a certain ordinance of reason, to the common good, from him who has care of the community, and promulgated."[42] Contained therein are four requirements for law, argued for in each of the articles on this question. For something to be a true law it must (1) pertain to reason, (2) be aimed at the common good, (3) originate from a lawgiver, and (4) be promulgated. Natural law as presented in Thomas's treatise must meet each of these requirements if it is to qualify as a genuine law, and to exclude any would make the natural law to be imperfect *qua* law. In particular, participation is indispensable for identifying how the natural law pertains to reason and originates from a lawgiver.

Employing the terminology of the first mode of participation, defining natural law as "nothing else than a participation of the eternal law in a rational creature" indicates both the genus of law as "participation in the eternal law"—that by which natural law is truly a *law*—and the specific difference as "in the rational creature"—that by which it is a *specific kind* of law. A law is not truly a law because it is *human* but rather because it is *rational*. That is, it is natural law's connection to the eternal law (and, Thomas shows, derivatively human law's connection to the natural law[43]) that renders the natural law to be a true law. Just as man is not the cause of his own being, so too the natural law is not the cause of its own legality. In Thomas's account it is the eternal law, not human rationality, that ultimately grounds all other forms of law. Furthermore, while for Thomas both natural law and human law are identified as kinds of participations in eternal law, the natural law is present *in* the participating creature and most properly within the rational creature. In this way, natural law falls under the genus of "participation in eternal law" and is specified by being present within the rational creature.[44] The first and second modes of participation thus show how natural law is rational and promulgated.

The third mode also directly relates to the origin of natural law. Natural law as a rational participation in eternal law is related to the eternal law in a relation of cause and effect. Understood in this way, there is direct and explicit reference to God as its origin. While Rhonheimer has attempted to promote a Thomistic definition of natural law that edits out reference to God as extraneous to the definition, this is not warranted by *Summa Theologiae*, I-II, q. 91. This bracketing of God (and, for that matter, exclusion of eternal law) is permissible, Rhonheimer claims, in the same way that defining an immaterial soul or creation need not include reference to God their creator.[45] Because he views the traditional definition merely as a description of the source of natural law, Rhonheimer holds that God and the eternal law ought not to figure in its formal definition. This comparison, however, does not hold. Thomas does not say that the essence of an immaterial soul or creation is the same as the essence of God. He does, however, say that the natural law *is* the eternal law, albeit as it exists in a rational creature.[46] It is true that reference to the source of a thing is not necessary to define it, but Thomas clearly identifies the natural law with the eternal law and, as such, the traditional definition does not merely describe its source. The natural law is the eternal law as it is in the rational creature (explicated by the first and second modes of participation) because it is an effect of the eternal law itself (third mode of participation). To omit reference to the eternal law from Thomas's definition of natural law would lose reference to its origin, the way it is promulgated, and the reason that enables it to be a genuine law. In this way, it would fail to meet the legal requirements established by Thomas in *Summa Theologiae*, I-II, q. 90. The promulgator of the natural law is expressly identified in the traditional definition's emphasis on the eternal law as cause.

That Thomas regards the natural and eternal law as true *laws* is clear by his own connecting of these laws to his general legal criteria within the treatise.[48] Without reference to the eternal law, though, many elements of law would not be met for the natural law. For this reason, then, the definition of natural law as participation of the rational creature in the eternal law is critical for conveying its full legality. Without a proper understanding of participation and the role it plays in uniting the natural law to the eternal law in rational creatures, the elements of law could not be included in the definition of natural law. This would, I propose, be inconsonant with Thomas's treatment of natural law in his treatise. Rhonheimer's favored definition of natural law as "the light of natural reason, whereby we discern what is good and what is evil" satisfies some of these elements, but not all of them. As such, it fails to account for the elements of law and cannot serve as the Thomistic definition. The traditional definition, on the other hand, when illuminated by an understanding of the meaning of "participation," is able to account for the legality of natural law and its relation to the eternal law.

Conclusion

To appreciate the richness of Thomas's treatise on law and his treatment of the natural law, one must consider the participation metaphysics he employs as well as its general legal context. It is through these that Thomas can account for the relation between natural law and eternal law and also satisfy his criteria for law. Without a proper understanding of participation and the role it plays in uniting the natural law to the eternal law in rational creatures, the elements of law could not be included in the definition of natural law. The question of whether or not natural law itself—not natural law as defined by Thomas—can or should be defined solely in terms of human reason is, of course, another issue. It is clear, however, that the Thomistic definition of natural law must reference the eternal law if it is to account for its legal character. Although many points of debate remain about both the natural law and Thomas's treatise, continued focus on participation and, in particular, its employment within *Summa Theologiae*, I-II, q. 90 are indispensable for understanding the meaning of the law written on our hearts.

Notes

1. Thomas Aquinas. *Summa Theologiae* [*ST*]. Rome: Commissio Leonina, 1882. *ST* I-II, q. 91, a. 2, c: "nihil aliud est quam participatio legis aeternae in rationali creatura." (VII, 153) Translations of Thomas's texts are my own.
2. Two exceptions to this general tendency are Craig A. Boyd's "Participation Metaphysics in Aquinas's Theory of Natural Law," *American Catholic Philosophical Quarterly* 79 (2005): 432-45; Boyd does not present Thomas's own teachings on participation and largely relies on the account of W. Norris Clarke and John Rziha's *Perfecting Human Actions: St. Thomas Aquinas on Human Participation in Eternal Law* (Washington, D.C.: The Catholic University of America Press, 2009). Martin Rhonheimer has also drawn attention to participation and the definition of natural law in his "Natural Law as a 'Work of Reason': understanding the metaphysics of participated theonomy," *American Journal of Jurisprudence* 55 (2010): 41-77. My critique of Rhonheimer's suggestion will be made in the course of the present study.
3. Notable studies include those of Cornelio Fabro, *La nozione metai.siea di partecipazione secondo S. d'Aquino*, and L.-B. Geiger, O.P., *La participation dans la philosophie de S. Thomas d'Aquin;* W. Norris Clarke, "The Meaning of Participation in St. Thomas," *Proceedings of the American Catholic Philosophical Association* (1952); the more recent work of Rudi Te Velde, *Participation and Substantiality in Thomas Aquinas*, and John Wippel, *The Metaphysical Thought of Thomas Aquinas*. The concern of these studies is focused on explicating the ontological significance of "participation," not a practical application, such as Thomas's treatise on law.
4. *ST*, I-II, a. 90, a. 4, c: "ex quatuor praedictis potest colligi definitio legis, quae nihil est

aliud quam quaedam rationis ordinatio ad bonum commune, ab eo qui curam communitatis habet, promulgata."

5. For example, *In libros Aristotelis De caelo et mundo expositio* II, lectio 18, n. 6 and in his *Super Epistolam B. Pauli ad Hebraeos lectura*, cap. VI, lectio 1.
6. See W. Norris Clarke, "The Meaning of Participation in St. Thomas," *Proceedings of the American Catholic Philosophical Association* (1952): 147-57, especially 152.
7. Thomas Aquinas, *Expositio libri Boetii de ebdomadibus.* Leonine Edition, volume 50: 232-96. Rome: Commissio Leonina, 1992; lectio 2: "Est autem participare quasi partem capere. Et ideo quando [1] aliquid particulariter recipit id quod ad alterum pertinet universaliter dicitur participare illud, sicut homo dicitur participare animal, quia non habet rationem animalis secundum totam communitatem... [2] Similiter etiam subiectum participat accidens et materia formam, quia forma substancialis uel accidentalis... [3] Et similiter etiam effectus dicitur participare sue causam, et praecipue quando non adaequat virtutem sue cause." Stephen Brock draws attention to Thomas also referencing a fourth mode of participation, that of the concrete in the universal, later in this same chapter: "sed id quod est, sive ens, quamvis sit communissimum, tamen concretive dicitur; et ideo participat ipsum esse, non per modum quo magis commune participatur a minus communi, sed participat ipsum esse per modum quo concretum participat abstractum." See Stephen Brock, "Harmonizing Plato and Aristotle on *Esse*: Thomas Aquinas and the *De hebdomadibus," Nova et Vetera,* English Edition 5 (2007): 465-94. This mode has particular pertinence for the way existence is signified, but it is introduced without examples and is at the same time the least important for the present study. I will, then, focus on the three principal modes presented within this commentary.
8. Thomas Aquinas. *Summa contra gentiles.* Leonine Edition, volume XIII. Rome: Commisio Leonina, 1882. *Summa contra gentiles,* I, 32: See also *ST,* I, q. 13, a. 5.
9. *ST,* I, q. 4, a. 3c: "illa quae sunt a Deo, assimilantur ei inquantum sunt entia, ut primo et universali principio totius esse." I mention this primarily to emphasize that creatures participate, but God does not. To explore further the intricacies and doctrine of Thomistic analogy lies beyond the purpose of the present study. I would argue, though, that an understanding of participation is also necessary if one is to understand Thomas's accounts.
10. *Expositio libri Boetii De ebdomadibus*, lectio 2: "Est autem participare quasi partem capere; et ideo quando aliquid particulariter recipit id quod ad alterum pertinet, universaliter dicitur participare illud[.]"
11. *Expositio libri Boetii De ebdomadibus*, lectio 2: "sicut homo dicitur participare animal, quia non habet rationem animalis secundum totam communitatem; et eadem ratione Socrates participat hominem[.]"
12. See *ST,* I-II, q. 93, a. 3c.
13. See especially ibid., q. 91, a. 1, ad 3 ("Sed finis divinae gubernationis est ipse Deus, nec eius lex est aliud ab ipso") and ibid. I, q. 3, a. 5).
14. Ibid., I-II, q. 93, a. 3, ad 2.
15. Ibid., q. 93, a. 3c.
16. Ibid., q. 91, a. 2, ad 1. This is because, as I will show in the body of this study, the participator is distinct from what is participated in.
17. See ibid. I-II, q. 91, a. 3, ad 1 & 3. For this reason, Thomas holds, man stands in need of laws in addition to the natural law. To one with an understanding of natural law as

participation, this should come as little surprise because finitude is implied in the notion of participation. Because of man's finiteness, the application of the natural law is likewise imperfect. As Thomas himself grants, participants in the eternal law, too, are prone to error (see ibid., I-II, q. 94, a. 5, ad 1).

18. Rhonheimer, "Natural Law as a 'Work of Reason,'" 43. This passage he is quoting is found within Thomas' commentary on the Decalogue, but a similar statement is found in the penultimate sentence of *ST* I-II, q. 91, a. 2: "quasi lumen rationis naturalis, quo discernimus quid sit bonum et malum."
19. Rhonheimer, "Natural Law as a 'Work of Reason,'" 53: "the very essence of natural law, and the focal meaning of the term 'natural law,' is not to be found in the last sentence of 1-2, 91, 2, but—to repeat it once more—in the preceding ones, briefly summarized in the most formal and focal definition of natural law as 'the light of natural reason, whereby we discern what is good and what is evil.'"
20. As Brock expresses this point, "the nature of man is no more the cause of the legality of natural law than it is the cause of its own being." See *The Legal Character of Natural Law According to St. Thomas Aquinas,* Doctoral Dissertation, University of Toronto, 1988, 84.
21. The passage from *ST,* I-II, q. 91 from which Rhonheimer draws this definition explicitly references God, but he edits this point out as unessential (see "Natural Law as a 'Work of Reason,'" 53). But even if he were correct in rejecting the traditional definition of natural law, it is not clear how he would solve this problem by relying on the previous sentence of this article. Indeed, the claim that natural law is the "light of natural reason" which is "nothing else than an imprint on us of the Divine Light" is susceptible to the same objections that he makes to the claim that natural law is a participation of the eternal law in a rational creature because Thomas explains both the "light of natural reason" and the "participation of the rational creature" by referencing their divine cause. The penultimate sentence of Thomas' text explicitly references God and, furthermore, the "light of natural reason" has been earlier identified as a participation in divine light: "Signatum est super nos lumen vultus tui, Domine, quasi lumen rationis naturalis, quo discernimus quid sit bonum et malum, quod pertinet ad naturalem legem, nihil aliud sit quam impressio divini luminis in nobis." (*ST,* I-II, q. 91, a. 2c; see also ST I, q. 12, a. 11, ad 3). This is not, of course, to dismiss the importance of Thomas's metaphor of natural and divine light. But for Thomas the light of natural reason is that "by which we discern what is good and what is evil" and this "pertains to natural law," while he reiterates that this light is itself "nothing other than the impression of divine light in us" (*ST,* I-II, q. 91, a. 2c). Substituting the light of natural reason for a definition of natural law thus neither separates it from divine light nor clarifies the relation between "light" and "law."
22. *Expositio libri Boetii de ebdomadibus*, lectio 2: "similiter etiam subiectum participat accidens, et materia formam, quia forma substantialis vel accidentalis, quae de sui ratione communis est, determinatur ad hoc vel ad illud subiectum[.]"Although the participation of subject and accident is given as an example, the focus of both the commentary and my present study is on the relation between matter and form.
23. See Brock, "Harmonizing Plato and Aristotle on *Esse*: Thomas Aquinas and the *De hebdomadibus*," 479. For Thomas's own explanation see *Expositio libri Boetii de ebdomadibus*, lectio 2.

24. *Quodlibet* XII, 5, 1c.
25. *ST,* I-II, q. 91, a. 2c: "sicut supra dictum est, lex, cum sit regula et mensura, dupliciter potest esse in aliquo, uno modo, sicut in regulante et mensurante; alio modo, sicut in regulato et mensurato, quia inquantum participat aliquid de regula vel mensura, sic regulatur vel mensuratur. Unde cum omnia quae divinae providentiae subduntur, a lege aeterna regulentur et mensurentur, ut ex dictis patet; manifestum est quod omnia participant aliqualiter legem aeternam, inquantum scilicet ex impressione eius habent inclinationes in proprios actus et fines."
26. For this reason he maintains that human law is necessary in addition to the natural law. See *ST,* I-II, q. 91, a. 2, ad 1.
27. *ST,* I-II, q. 91, a. 2, c.
28. Ibid., q. 91, a. 2, ad 3: "etiam animalia irrationalia participant rationem aeternam suo modo, sicut et rationalis creatura. Sed quia rationalis creatura participat eam intellectualiter et rationaliter, ideo participatio legis aeternae in creatura rationali proprie lex vocatur: nam lex est aliquid rationis...In creatura autem irrationali non participatur rationaliter: unde non potest dici lex nisi per similitudinem." See also ibid., q. 93, a. 5, c.
29. *Expositio libri Boetii de ebdomadibus,* l. 2.
30. See *ST,* I, q. 2, a. 1.
31. See ibid., I-II, q. 94, a. 6.
32. Ibid., q. 93, a. 2c.
33. This solar example is a favorite of Thomas, as he also uses it in his commentary on the *De ebdomadibus* as a way to explain the third mode of participation.
34. *ST,* I, q. 2, a. 1, c.
35. *Questiones disputatae de potentia Dei.* Marietti edition, volume 11:1-276. Rome: Marietti, 1939.q. 3, a. 5, ad 1.
36. As Clifford Kossel notes, this method "is Aquinas's normal procedure in all matters concerned with God. The proofs for His existence are quia proofs (effect to cause) and proofs for all other attributes (except those known only through divine revelation) depend on those proofs along with other observations about the nature of the effects." See his "Natural Law and Human Law" in *The Ethics of Aquinas*, ed. Stephen J. Pope (Washington, D.C.: Georgetown University Press, 2002), 184n22.
37. John Rziha puts this point in *Perfecting Human Actions: St. Thomas Aquinas on Human Participation in Eternal Law*, 105n244: "natural law has its own intelligibility without explicit knowledge of the eternal law. Nonetheless, for perfect understanding of the natural law, the eternal law must be known." It is, perhaps, more accurate to speak of "better" or "more complete" understanding of an effect rather than "perfect" understanding because, according to Thomas, "cognitio enim contingit secundum quod cognitum est in cognoscente. Cognitum autem est in cognoscente secundum modum cognoscentis" (*ST,* I, q. 12, a. 4c). Unless man is a perfect knower, then, his knowledge will not be perfect. To address this issue is beyond the scope of this paper, but referring to "more complete" knowledge of an effect can maintain Thomas' point of the perfecting of knowledge gained through knowledge of a cause while avoiding epistemological issues raised by claiming "perfect" knowledge.
38. A charge Rhonheimer has levied at Long; see Rhonheimer, "Natural Law as a 'Work of Reason,'" 52-53.

39. Steven Long, "Natural Law or Autonomous Practical Reason: Problems for the New Natural Law Theory," in *St Thomas Aquinas and the Natural Law Tradition: Contemporary Perspectives*, eds. John Goyette, Mark Latkovic, and Richard S. Myers, 65-193 (Washington, DC: The Catholic University of America Press, 2004), 191.
40. Kossel presents this point in "Natural Law and Human Law," 172: "the knowledge of natural law and human law does not depend on the knowledge of God or eternal law, but vice versa." He continues, however, to state that "this does not exclude the requirement of a 'reduction' to the ultimate causes for an adequate *understanding* of law." In this way, Long can also hold that natural law is a precondition for the exercise of practical reason, being "the normative theological and metaphysical order that undergirds, makes possible, and flows into our moral order" (see Long, "Natural Law or Autonomous Practical Reason," 166). Rhonheimer disagrees with Long on this point at 65-66. To adapt Long's metaphor to the order of discovery, the natural law could be compared to an opera with the eternal law as composer. We can hear and understand the singers but without the composer their performance would not constitute an opera. Maintaining that one needs a composer for an opera in no way renders the singers irrelevant. Indeed, for there to be an opera (natural law) at all there must be both a composer (eternal law) and performers (human participation). In this way, we can understand natural law as an effect without explicit awareness of the eternal law as its cause, though we are drawn from effects to their cause.
41. Although not directly addressing the points I raise in this study, Craig Boyd also emphasizes the importance of participation in Thomas's account for natural law. In particular, he addresses the position of Anthony Lisska (whom Rhonheimer approvingly references in "Natural Law as a 'Work of Reason,'" 53) who holds that God can be eliminated from accounts of natural law. Boyd also discuss the position of D'Entreves, who claims that natural law is unintelligible apart from an understanding of its connection with the eternal law. See Craig A. Boyd, "Participation Metaphysics in Aquinas's Theory of Natural Law," *American Catholic Philosophical Quarterly* 79 (2005): 432-45.
42. *ST,* I-II, a. 90, a. 4, c.
43. See ibid., q. 95, a. 2.
44. Ibid., q. 91, a. 2, ad 1: "ratio illa procederet, si lex naturalis esset aliquid diversum a lege aeterna. Non autem est nisi quaedam participatio eius, ut dictum est."
45. Rhonheimer, "Natural Law as a 'Work of Reason,'" 53: "I have put the phrase 'infused in us by God' into parenthesis, because it is not necessary for the definition of the essence of natural law, just as creation by God of the spiritual soul is not to be included into the definition of the essence of spiritual soul, or creation of nature by God into the definition of 'nature.'"
46. *ST,* I-II, q. 91, a. 2, ad 1. See also I-II, q. 91, a. 3, ad 1: "humana non potest participare ad plenum dictamen rationis divinae, sed suo modo et imperfecte."
47. See ibid., q. 90, a. 4, ad 1.
48. The eternal law fulfills the requirements that law *pertains to reason* and *originates from a lawgiver* together, as Thomas explains in the body of *ST,* I-II, q. 91, a. 1. Eternal law is also *aimed at the common good* precisely because "mundus divina providentia regatur, ut in primo habitum est, quod tota communitas universi gubernatur ratione divina" (*ST* I-II, q. 91, a. 1c). Finally, Thomas also explains the *promulgation* of the eternal law in the second reply of *ST* I-II, q. 91, a. 1: "dicendum quod promulgatio fit

et verbo et scripto; et utroque modo lex aeterna habet promulgationem ex parte Dei promulgantis, quia et verbum divinum est aeternum, et Scriptura libri vitae est aeterna. Sed ex parte creaturae audientis aut inspicientis, non potest esse promulgatio aeterna." The natural law *pertains to reason* and *originates from a lawgiver* are claims defended within this study. One should note even now, though, that Thomas himself explicitly invokes his requirement that *law pertain to reason* when distinguishing the participation of man from other beings at *ST* I-II, q. 91, a. 2, ad 3. Thomas also explicitly, albeit briefly, addresses the question of natural law's *promulgation* in *ST* I-II, q. 90, a. 4, ad 1. He returns to this point and explains it at greater length in *ST* I-II, q. 94, a. 4 when discussing whether the natural law is known to all. The requirement that law be *aimed at the common good* is likewise relevant to Thomas's presentation of the precepts of the natural law in *ST* I-II, q. 94, a. 2c.

Review of *Natural Law Today: The Present State of the Perennial Philosophy*
Edited by Christopher Wolfe and Steven Brust (Lanham, MD: Lexington Books, 2018)

Matthew Minerd

In this volume, the reader is presented with a number of thoughtful and thought-provoking essays regarding the metaphysical foundations of the natural law, its overall epistemological character, and its continual (and continued) historical importance. Drawing together essays by a number of well-known authors on these matters, the volume provides a kind of primer regarding the current "state of the art" on these topics, in particular as they are discussed by thinkers who are significantly indebted to the Thomistic conceptual register in matters of natural law, though not exclusively so. As will be seen below, I think very highly of this volume and recommend it warmly to the readers of *Lex Naturalis*. However, let us turn to my particular comments on each essay, whereby I will present the details of this positive judgment.

Steven Long's opening essay undertakes a reflection on the natural law as the structuring principle of moral reasoning as such. As he has done in other works, he emphasizes the fact that practical reason receives its "spending capital…from the divine ordering of creation" (10). Without falling into a facile naturalism regarding the derivation of the natural law, Long clearly stands in the line of those whose voice inflects heavily on the fact that the authority of the natural law is extrinsic to human reason, objectively measuring it, and maintaining its connection to natural teleology. Given that Long writes from within an openly Thomist perspective, the reader may wish for him to present more detailed reflections on the precise connection point between the natural law and our first, most basic human knowledge thereof, namely the *per se nota* knowledge we have through synderesis. Alas, while such reflections are not presented to the reader, we are rewarded nonetheless by an admirable closing to this essay, which emphasizes a point that is often underemphasized among proponents of natural law morality, namely, the fact that for Thomas and the Thomists the fundamental inclination of the rational creature is that by which he or she is ordered to the First Cause. Thus, as one glimpses in Aristotle and sees very clearly in Aquinas, the virtue of religion remains the capstone of the virtue of justice (and, thereby, of the moral virtues), and as Long states with great perspicuity, "When this rational inclination is diminished, the whole ethical life shivers with the tremors of alienation" (13).

One could pair Long's essay with a text later in the volume, namely Hadley Arkes's "The Natural Law—Again, Ever." Indeed, among all the essays in this admirable volume, this text is perhaps the shining gem. Writing in a very honest, non-dogmatic, philosophical tone, Arkes takes up a theme dear to his heart (but also to the hearts of all defenders of the natural law), namely, the fact that the very practice of legal reasoning constantly forces us to go beyond the posited texts lying at the basis of jurisprudential reasoning, "going beyond the text…to those premises, or principles, that were antecedent to the text" (117). His discussion of *per se nota* self-evidence is admirable, especially because he notes that well-known point made by Aquinas (and a number of Thomists): self-evidence is not equal for all. In other words, there are things that are *per se nota* only for the wise. (Along these lines, actually, Maritain in his *Loi naturelle, loi non écrite* notes the importance of understanding this point so that one can thereby understand how we historically grow in our knowledge of the natural law.) Arkes is writing from an American perspective, and he cites on pages 122-24 some fascinating passages from our founders regarding self-evident maxims, bearing witness to the resonances of late scholasticism in modern thought. The end of the essay stirringly shows through repeated examples how the deniers of natural law in fact stand in need of such self-evident bases if their own often-strenuously-proclaimed claims are to be more than ultimately relativistic protestations. Again, I think that the volume is worth purchasing if only for this honest and thoughtful essay.

Directly following Long's first essay in the volume is Michael Pakaluk's "Natural Inclinations in Aquinas's Account of Natural Law." Given the famed texts in *Summa Theologiae*, I-II concerning the natural inclinations which lie at the basis of the natural law, this study provides useful interpretive fleshing-out of the meaning of *inclinatio* in Aquinas. Of particular use here is his careful distinction of *inclinatio* from desire. Likewise, his brief discussion of the knowledge of these inclinations both in a speculative manner and a practical manner provides insightful pointers for further considerations of the warp and woof of moral epistemology.

Unlike many of the other studies in this volume, Fulvio Di Blasi's essay steers the reader's attention toward historical matters regarding the notions of *ius naturale* and *lex naturalis*. He notes well the shift in modern thought leading to an understanding of the natural law as a basic claim or freedom to be taken into account by the political community, and while acknowledging the benefits drawn from this development, he is also well aware that "the current crisis concerning the basis of, and the international agreement about, human rights is a powerful reminder of the unavoidable problem of their being somehow natural or not" (40). Moreover, his brief remarks on *ius naturale* from the perspective of the activity of justice draws on some important themes in scholasticism (namely, without using the terms, the distinction between a *medium rationis tantum* and a *medium rei*), noting well the ways that this is related (though not equivalent) to the Kantian distinction between the moral law and positive law. (Much development is needed here, given the pliability even within the domain of those actions which have a *medium rei*. But only so much can be done in one essay!) Finally, he ends with a pedagogically helpful summary of what are commonly called "New Natural Law" theories.

Later in the volume, J. Daryl Charles provides a very enlightening historical essay regarding the issue of natural law thought in Protestantism. Given certain themes in Barthian theology, as well as the work of influential Protestant thinkers like Hauerwas, it is tempting to think that little room is left for discussing natural law theory in a Protestant milieu. Moreover, I must admit that my general bias has been to think that, in the end, Protestant thought falls prey to the voluntarism of late scholasticism, basically cutting it off from "real" natural law reflection. Alas, what an ignorant thought on my part, given that there were so many famed Natural Law thinkers in Protestant Scholasticism! It is good to have such a corrective as this essay. In any case, alongside clear-headed summaries of the anti-Natural Law tendencies of thinkers like Barth, Hauerwas, Ellul, Yoder, and Niebuhr, the author presents the ways Luther, Calvin, Zwingli, and Bullinger accepted the possibility of natural moral reasoning, even while taking up their well-known positions regarding the damages suffered by human nature through the Fall. Charles makes a convincing case from a Protestant perspective that "[l]aw is not some creative luxury or a sort of second-tier theological speculation; nor is it solely the domain of 'grace-denying' Catholics. Rather, it is of the order of necessity and consequently must be at the heart of Christian theological speculation" (102). This Catholic reviewer gladly welcomes the fruits of continued discussions along these lines, which will doubtlessly bring much fruit to discussions of natural law.

Budziszewski's essay "The Same as to Knowledge" reflects on what we might call the psychological problem of denial of the natural law. In this well-written text, he explains what is meant by the claim that the natural law is the same for all as regards knowledge of the law. Through a series of objections and responses, he defends the claim that even those who choose wrongly have the natural disposition for knowing the principles of natural law as well as their basic corollaries. (Here again, the reader wishes for some study of the nature of synderesis in medieval and late-medieval thought, which may help to clarify some of these difficulties as well.) Wading into slightly controversial waters, he uses a number of examples from the domain of abortion to spell out how such natural knowledge of basic moral precepts may be displaced into other forms of "moral avoidance." It would be interesting for such points to be documented in a number of psychological domains, cataloguing the various ways that moral self-deception can take place. (Moreover, such detailed psychological studies would help to confirm the classical theories of such *per se nota* knowledge.) Finally, Budziszewski closes with a spot-on reflection regarding the vocation of the philosopher and the moral commitments necessary for truly following this vocation in all honesty. It is quite an appropriately Socratic ending to a thoughtful essay, which we have all come to expect from Budziszewski's pen.

Brust's essay "Aquinas's Second Reason for the Necessity of the Divine Law" takes up an important theme in Christian theories of natural law, namely the relationship between the naturally normative law and the law of grace. Although it seems that Brust on several occasions treats the New Law of Grace in terms of its external teaching (when, in fact, it is precisely the action of divinization through grace and secondarily its written forms), he rightly emphasizes its internal character as well. On the whole, nonetheless, the essay presents something that is vitally important for understanding Aquinas (and many other Christian authors) appropriately on these matters. According to Christian theorists, our human encounter with natural moral normativity is embedded within the broader context of the Fall and the Redemption. Brust asserts the need for the divine law for even knowing the natural law, given the frailties of human existence, and while some readers may be opposed to these claims, I am generally in agreement with his sage points to this end: "The focus of 'unaided' reason, while necessary is not sufficient, and a neglect of divine law leaves society (and the individual) in an inadequate state" (81). Indeed, the whole section "Contemporary Circumstances" presents an admirable reflection on this important theme.

Christopher Wolfe's essay "Thomas Aquinas's Concept of Natural Law: A Guide to Healthy Liberalism" is primarily concerned with the second half of the title. His overall concern is to acknowledge the positive relations that natural law reasoning and liberalism can have with each other. He is well aware of the weaknesses inherent in the modern liberal outlook, and reflection on this fact makes up no small part of the essay's opening. He notes the troublesome relationship of individual rights to the regime as such (which for the liberal will ever appear as being an instrumental, socially-constructed means for the acquisition of conditions for individual flourishing). Likewise, he reflects on the relativism about human flourishing that bedevils liberal thought, as well as the troubled relationship that liberal regimes have in relation to revealed religion and also to the family as a pre-existing institution with its own unique duties and rights. Only after acknowledging these weaknesses, he presents brief but thoughtful reflections on how the tradition of natural law liberalism can help "preserve liberalism from its own worst tendencies" (147). While I personally am somewhat more skeptical about liberal political theory, I found Wolfe's essay to be a thoughtful and honest reflection on the difficulties at hand between natural law reasoning and liberal political thought.

The volume concludes with a text posthumously drawn from the works of Ralph McInerny, the long-time defender of many perennial philosophical topics. Lovers of traditional philosophy owe much to McInerny's lifelong work at Notre Dame. This essay has all of his characteristic charm, recounting the fate of natural law thought during his long career. He notes the passage in the Catholic world from the days of Thomist confidence to an era soon after the Second Vatican Council when "you could shoot a cannon through a Catholic campus and not hit a Thomist" (154). He then provides a very brief discussion of the changed environment during this period of Thomist "diaspora" from the 1960s-1990, closing with avuncular advice to those present to not fear to philosophize as Catholic thinkers, keeping well the distinction between philosophy and theology but also following the maxim of Maritain, drawn from John of St. Thomas: *philosophandum in fide*.

I highly recommend this volume for the reflection of those who are well-trained in matters philosophical and also as a text to be used for upper-level undergraduate courses as well as for graduate school courses focusing on the current state of discussions among various branches of the natural law reflection.

Review of *Why Liberalism Failed*
by Patrick J. Deneen (Yale University Press, 2018)

James M. Jacobs

Forty years ago, Alexander Solzhenitsyn gave a Commencement Address at Harvard that has proved as prophetic as it was incisive. The Russian surprised his audience, for instead of extolling the liberal democracies for being a bulwark of freedom against Soviet tyranny, he criticized their decline into moral lassitude, a decline he blamed on "humanistic autonomy: the proclaimed and practiced autonomy of man from any higher force above him....It started modern Western civilization on the dangerous trend of worshiping man and his material needs." In the decades since 1978, Western liberalism's policies have only exacerbated those materialistic and individualistic tendencies. This privileging of material satiety over man's spiritual fulfillment, however, has bred a profound dissatisfaction and has led ineluctably to the various illiberal reactions, from Trump to Brexit to Orban, which have elicited such histrionic responses from the now anxious liberal panjandrums.

Patrick Deneen's *Why Liberalism Failed* is a timely diagnosis of the current state of moral disorder arising from our disregard for timeless truths. Deneen is an astute critic, drawing broadly on both philosophy and the data of the social sciences to demonstrate that liberalism was doomed from the start, for its faulty premises about human nature and society undermine its ability to fulfill its promise of universal happiness.

While Deneen only mentions *natural law* explicitly three times, his argument rests on the truths of natural law, for Deneen believes that it is liberalism's repudiation of those principles that has caused its death. Liberalism's faulty anthropology, in which freedom is seen as liberating man from the constraints of nature, inevitably distorts its social order, for government now exists only to protect the rights of autonomous individuals to pursue their own idea of the good. Already in this idea of freedom is the seed of destruction sown, for such autonomous individuals cannot form a society united in a common good. As Deneen states in his thesis, "As liberalism has 'become more truly itself,' as its inner logic has become more evident and its self-contradictions manifest, it has generated pathologies that are at once deformations of its claims yet realizations of liberal ideology" (3).

Those contradictions and pathologies arise most fundamentally from its distortion of human nature. While liberalism claims to be neutral with respect to metaphysical and moral commitments, it insidiously inculcates a materialism and voluntarism that deprive life of spiritual significance. For the sake of freedom, it systematically destroys the traditional social relations of family, church, and polis, disembedding the individual from nature and society and depriving him of the opportunity to develop virtue. These ideological changes are manifested in four areas—politics, economics, education, and technology—in which the overweening intervention of authority perpetually reshapes man's desires in order to overturn the natural moral and political order.

The first chapter, "Unsustainable Liberalism" (an expanded version of Deneen's well-known *First Things* essay from 2012) presents the philosophical context for liberalism's departure from the natural law tradition. The original sin of liberalism is its understanding of liberty: instead of freedom arising from virtuous self-mastery in accord with natural law, liberty is now seen to be the satisfaction of desires unconstrained by law. Because this sort of freedom is man's birthright, the aim of government is to further that freedom by destroying all "irrational religious and social norms" that stand in the way of individual pursuit. All social relations are now subject to consent, the only remaining moral criterion for autonomous individuals. Deneen sees the development of liberalism as characterized by these three "basic revolutions of thought, redefining liberty as the liberation of humans from established authority, emancipation from arbitrary culture and tradition, and the expansion of human power and dominion over nature through advancing scientific discovery and economic prosperity" (27). Liberalism, then, will aim to solve all ills by constantly extending personal autonomy abetted by bureaucracy and technology, at the expense of family, community, church, and nation.

The subsequent chapters develop the consequences of a society built upon individuals who are liberated from all "gratitude to the past and obligations to the future" (39). The first and most ironic of these is the symbiosis between individualism and statism: In a society lacking common moral norms, the state must expand to police all relations. The more the state and the market succeed in liberating individuals from social limitations, from culture and community, the more those individuals will be dependent on the state for guidance and assistance. A community deprived the guidance of natural law necessarily takes its orders from the positive law; the state becomes the only thing the mass of individuals have in common.

The antagonism of liberalism to man's rootedness in community and nature is perhaps best illustrated in its deleterious effects on education. Traditional liberal education nurtured free persons who learned virtue through engagement with the tradition. This has been replaced by a servile education which "makes liberal individuals servants to the end of untutored appetites, restlessness, and technical mastery of the natural world" (111). The STEM fields yield ever greater control of nature and so ever greater "freedom" from arbitrary constraints. In their pathetic quest to remain relevant, the humanities politicize themselves to give the illusion that they, too, can help the student harness the will to power. This education—utilitarian and utopian, devoid of the influence of community and culture—produces a new technocratic global elite who are empowered to reshape the world.

This process of homogeneous individualization then recursively debases the notion of democratic citizenship. Democracy, as the American Founders knew, could only be the province of a virtuous and religious people. But in liberalism, democracy has come to be associated with an amoral expressive individualism for private citizens, which cedes public responsibility to the state. Thus, Deneen comments, "As long as liberal democracy expands 'the empire of liberty,' mainly in the form of expansive rights, power, and wealth, the actual absence of active democratic self-rule is not only an acceptable but desired end" (155). Having despaired of the self-governance that is the fruit of virtue, liberals have now surrendered political self-determination to a distant and unaccountable bureaucracy which survives by promising ever more material benefit. But, as Plato knew, a people united in the pursuit of pleasure paves the way for tyranny.

Deneen's concluding response to this sorry state is to argue that we must develop not simply a better political theory, but also concrete political practices based on metaphysically grounded ideas of human liberty and dignity. This is a great challenge, since liberalism has already "ruthlessly drawn down a reservoir of both material and moral resources that [we] cannot replenish" (18). The danger is that, in the absence of objective values, we would fall for another ideology, another utopian prescription that undermines both the family and the polis. Thus, Deneen, like Heinrich Rommen and Alasdair MacIntyre before him, recognizes that we must now expectantly await the eternal return of the natural law.

Review of *The Natural Law Reader*

Edited by Jacqueline A. Laing and Russell Wilcox (Oxford: Wiley Blackwell Publishing, 2014)

Scott J. Roniger

The editors of *The Natural Law Reader*, Jacqueline A. Laing and Russell Wilcox, have undertaken a difficult task and done an admirable job completing it. They have assembled a collection of texts that illustrates "the intellectual wealth of natural law thinking in the Western world" (1). It is to their credit that they identify the thought of St. Thomas Aquinas as a touchstone for natural law thinking, one that orients their selection of texts. With Aquinas serving as the central representative of the western, Judeo-Christian intellectual tradition of natural law thinking, Laing and Wilcox are able to unify their project by choosing texts that "in some way or other" illuminate or contribute to "the central tradition" expressed in Aquinas's writings (4). Further, they are to be commended not only for making principled selections but also for making the principles of their selections manifest, thereby disclosing something of the method or process that animates their work of selection and unification. They say clearly that their selection of texts for the reader "is not, then, a neutral selection" (3). Indeed, one doubts whether any selection could be "neutral" (if there could be a neutral one, would such neutrality be desirable?), especially given the bipartite Thomistic teaching that all human agents are naturally oriented toward good (and away from evil) but that these rational inclinations must be shaped by a decent upbringing, to say nothing of additional Divine assistance, if they are to bear the fruit of happiness in the life of virtue. Naturally oriented toward the good, human agents see the world through the lens of their acquired character, and therefore an attempt at a "neutral" collection would be unnatural. It is therefore interesting to note that their method of selection and collection, as well as their explicit manifestation of this method, reveals something about the reality discussed by the texts selected and collected. Both the collection and the method itself of collecting show something about the natural law tradition highlighted in the collection.

The Natural Law Reader is a handsome volume in which Laing and Wilcox enumerate four main sections entitled as follows: (1) General Introduction (pp. 1-4); (2) Historical Readings, ranging from Heraclitus to the twentieth-century Dominican theologian Servais Pinckaers (pp. 5-250); (3) Contemporary Natural Law, in which fundamental issues of natural law theory are discussed by contemporary thinkers (pp. 251-366); (4) Applied Natural Law, in which principles are deployed to discuss issues such as contraception and human rights (pp. 367-445).

One small criticism is that this official division of the text leaves something to be desired. It would have been better, because more congruent with the *de facto* structure of the themes and readings, to divide the collection into two main parts (Historical Readings and Contemporary Natural Law), with each part further subdivided. However, the texts selected and collected provide a deep reservoir of natural law thinking, and the near equal space provided to (a) classic discussions of the natural law and (b) contemporary expositions of the law of nature creates an interesting, fruitful, and dynamic tension between the sources of natural law thinking and their deployment and development in recent years. In addition to the selected texts, Laing and Wilcox supply a brief introduction for each of the subsections. The collection is therefore a great boon for professors and students, and it should provide an excellent resource both for scholarship and teaching undergraduate and graduate courses on the natural law tradition.

Before closing, I wish to make an observation and a suggestion. The issue of the *promulgation* of the natural law is woefully underdeveloped throughout the collection. This observation is not, however, a criticism of Laing and Wilcox except *per accidens*, for it is precisely their fidelity to the natural law tradition culminating in Aquinas that leads to this lacuna. Aquinas holds that promulgation is of the very essence of law, not merely one of its *per se* properties, but he says very little about how the natural law is promulgated, and his contemporary commentators say even less. The selection from

Alasdair MacIntyre's essay "Theories of Natural Law in the Culture of Advanced Modernity" (363-66) comes closest to an insightful discussion of the issue of promulgation. In order to understand the importance of promulgation, one must see the natural law both from the side of the legislator and from the side of the "recipient," the one measured by the law; the promulgation of natural law includes both the giving and the discovering of the law.

In order to fill this thematic gap, the editors would do well to consider including the work of Francis Slade and Robert Sokolowski in any future edition. Slade and Sokolowski distinguish between natural ends and human purposes, and in light of this distinction they show that the natural law can be understood as the ontological priority of ends over human purposes. It is therefore in the drawing of this distinction and the recognition of the priority of natural ends over the purposes or intentions of the agent that one discovers the natural law. Such a discussion sheds light on the issue of promulgation and would help to complete the collection. Indeed, the editors themselves fail to make the distinction between ends and purposes. In the introduction to the well-selected texts from the ancient period, Laing and Wilcox say, "Aristotle's metaphysics and his ethics supply a foundation for the universality and timelessness of the natural law. His teleological approach holds things to be designed from or directed toward *an end or purpose. This end or purpose* is sometimes referred to as a thing's 'final cause'" (9). Ends are not synonymous with purposes, and the failure to make this distinction leads to a failure to disclose how the natural law is discovered and hence promulgated.

In closing, let us imitate Aquinas's method, itself an imitation of the created order, by returning to our beginning discussion of the method employed by the editors. Laing and Wilcox reveal to the reader their method of selection and comment upon what is selected, but what is selected and the commentary on it do not reveal the natural "method" of discovering what is discussed by the selection and commentary: the natural law. Again, the work of the editors reveals something important about the tradition they wish to introduce to the reader.

The American Maritain Association Notepad

Gregory Kerr, DeSales University

Readers of *Lex Naturalis* may be very interested in the philosophical conversations taking place in the American Maritain Association. A caveat is in order before I begin. Since the international meetings of the American Maritain Association contain a treasure trove of papers given in concurrent sessions, I actually experience quite a small amount of each conference. I can, therefore only provide a small taste of what it was like.

Before I report on any of the recent meetings, however, let me point the reader to two valuable web resources where there is much conversation. First, there is the American Maritain Association website where you can find the latest news and past history about our meetings, call for papers, and publications. This website also has two videos from plenary sessions from our 2017 Conference in New Orleans, that of Fr. Stephen Brock of the Pontifical University of the Holy Cross on "Aquinas the Conservationist" and Dr. Eleonore Stump of St. Louis University on "The God of the Bible and the God of the Philosophers." For anyone wanting to explore the interchange between Biblical faith and philosophy, this latter lecture is a Godsend. It is at https://maritainassociation.com. So if you are new to or a veteran of natural law theory or even perennial philosophy in general and interested in how it engages the contemporary world, be sure to check out this website and read our latest free online newsletters. And, by the way, we are always looking for new members and contributors.

The second website to mention is the well-established Jacques Maritain Center (1957) at the University of Notre Dame. It is at https://maritain.nd.edu. The center has quite an extensive collection of works by and about Maritain as well as other major thinkers. If you are looking for any title linked to Maritain and his views on natural law, this might be your first resource. I love pointing out to students that there are many free online ebooks of

Maritain's published works available here as well as many entire articles from authors in published collections that had their beginnings in AMA conference papers.

Our 2018 conference in Philadelphia, hosted by St. Charles Borromeo Seminary, was on "Thomism and Science" and it included the first meeting of our International Natural Law Society. We were very honored to have the Rev. Joseph Koterski, S.J., of Fordham University (and a teacher of natural law for the famous *The Great Courses* series, which can be found at https://www.thegreatcourses.com/courses/natural-law-and-human-nature.html), talking about "Distinguishing Principles and Prudential Judgments in Catholic Social Teaching" and James Jacobs (the AMA program director for the conferences) of Notre Dame Seminary, New Orleans, presenting on "Transcendental Love and the Natural Law."

During the conference, there was an amazing snowstorm outside and quite a storm inside our hotel with such key speakers such as the intellectually stimulating Rev. Robert Spitzer, S.J. (25th President of Gonzaga University and current president of the *Magis Center*, https://www.magiscenter.com/) on "Evidence for God from Physics and Philosophy: Extending the Legacy of St. Thomas Aquinas and Monsignor Georges Lemaître." I found his engagement with the thought of Stephen Hawking quite illuminating. (Hint: the math doesn't work out for a stable multiverse—there had to be a beginning!) Anthony Rizzi of the *Institute for Advanced Physics* gave his presentation on "The Real Conflict between Science, Morality and the Faith: Why are we losing on every front? We have found the enemy and he is us!" He argued that our culture had abandoned the realist foundation of physics and this has tremendous reverberating consequences for every dimension of our lives with regard to our appreciation of objective laws irrespective of our individual perspectives. Other topics included the theories of DeKoninck, Aquinas and contemporary psychology, Maritain and Einstein, Snake Evolution (why evolution actually allows God to create a greater variety of species), Yves R. Simon, Thomism and pragmatism, semiotics, MacIntyre, St. John Paul II, Stanley Jaki, Marx, Heidegger, Sartre, Peirce,

Charles Taylor, contemporary neuroscience, John Locke, Thomas Jefferson, Leo Strauss, and a session on the legacy of John Deely. And buried within all of the science and philosophy papers was a gem of a paper by Stephen Chamberlain of Rockhurst University entitled "Literary Knowledge: Story as a Kind of Science." This has especial significance to *Lex Naturalis* readers as it is a fascinating analysis of Aristotle's notion of the intellectual virtue of *synesis* (understanding) and how it relates to literature and aesthetic and moral knowledge. Look for this in the future!

The 2019 conference on *Thomism and Theology* was held, thanks to DeSales University, at the DeSales University Center in Center Valley, Pennsylvania. And if the former conference was a bit of a storm, the latter mirrored the peaceful campus of DeSales, where Dr. James Jacobs had no small help from master venue planner, Dr. Joshua Schulz.

There was much discussion on the nature of the relationship between philosophy and theology and the history of the changing relationship between the two. Is there a Christian philosophy? Would a purely natural philosophy still be helpful to theology? On Friday morning we heard from Sara Hulse of DeSales University on "Reason as Gift: Henri de Lubac on the Question of Christian Philosophy." We also heard from a prize-winning philosophy student at DeSales, Anton Schauble, in "A Christian Philosophy? Theologies of Nature and Grace and the Relationship between Philosophy and Revelation" that sparked a lively discussion on "*esse*." And we heard from Anne Frances Ai Le, OP, from the University of St. Thomas (Houston) on "Jacques Maritain, The Reluctant Thomist Theologian?"

We were also treated to separate histories of the development of the relation of philosophy to theology in the twentieth century: the role and importance of Blondel (author of *L'Action*) to theology and the significance of the development of the Lublin school of theology. Jon Kirwan of St. Patrick's Seminary gave a fascinating account of the dynamic philosophy of Blondel and of his suitability for theology in "Ambroise Gardeil, Garrigou Lagrange, and Maurice Blondel: A First Engagement (1896-1910)." Brian Panasiak of the John Paul II

Catholic University of Lublin spoke on the history and development of Lublin Thomism in Poland in "Lublin Thomism as a Basis for John Paul II's *Theology of the Body* and Social Theology." Both papers were engaging historical accounts of philosophy's key role in aiding and forming theological concepts.

Plenary papers were given by Dominic Legge, OP, of the Dominican House of Studies on "The Mind of Christ: Christ's Human Knowledge and Our Salvation" and Thomas Weinandy, OFM Cap., of the International Theological Commission, on "Jacques Maritain: Incarnational Humanism." The question of whether the intellect or the will should have priority was central for both thinkers who were in disagreement. Also presenting plenary papers were Siobhan Nash-Marshall of Manhattanville College on "Job, Aquinas, and the Problem of Evil" and John F. X. Knasas of the University of St. Thomas (Houston) on "Thomism and Theology: *Fides et Ratio* and the Wishes of St. John Paul II," and as a panel, Christopher Grey of the Open University (UK), John Trapani, Jr. of Walsh University (Emeritus) and myself (DeSales) all had fun presenting on "Understanding Music Truthfully: What Maritain Might Have Said." And with Christopher Grey's presentation, we were treated to a delightful musical demonstration of and commentary on the music of Bach.

Perhaps the plenary talk that nicely highlighted some of the central questions of the conference was that of D. C. Schindler of the Pontifical John Paul II Institute and his "Guardians of Metaphysics: The Christian Task in the Twenty-First Century." He highlighted the necessity of doing metaphysics and of continually asking such questions as What is it? What is being? and What is human excellence? Civilization began by asking such questions. Today Christians and others tend to reduce things to practical terms. From Bacon and Galileo on, there was the programmatic dismissal of the "what is" question in favor of the "how does it work" question. To compound the problem, modern logic excludes the "what is" question; however, civilization needs to know what is at the heart of things. According to Hans Urs von Balthasar, the Christian is called to be the guardian of metaphysics.

And, in addition to the above papers, our programs annually present the Presidential Address from James Hanink, who insightfully reminds us about the most important and fundamental principles necessary for doing philosophy. And perhaps the next time a program appears for the conference in March of 2020, might we see the title of your presentation there?

CONTRIBUTORS

Julia Bolzon is a doctoral candidate at the Pontifical John Paul II Institute in Washington D.C., studying the philosophical and theological foundations of the human person, marriage, and family. Her research focuses on the philosophical underpinnings of bioethics in America and the contribution of Hans Jonas.

Megan Furman is a doctoral candidate in Philosophy at the Institute of Philosophic Studies, University of Dallas. Having received her B.A. in English with a minor in Italian from the University of Notre Dame, a M.A. in English from St. Anne's College, Oxford, and M.A. degrees in philosophy and theology from the Dominican School of Philosophy and Theology in Berkeley, Furman has published on beauty, moral philosophy, and artistic creativity. In ten years of work in international affairs, she authored three texts and contributed to three documentary films on the Sultanate of Oman. Now at the University of Dallas, she is working in comparative philosophies of language, ancient, modern, and contemporary.

James M. Jacobs is Professor of Philosophy and Assistant Academic Dean at Notre Dame Seminary in New Orleans, LA, where he has taught since 2003. He holds a B.A. from Harvard University and a Ph.D. from Fordham University. His major area of research is Thomistic natural law theory and more generally the need for philosophical realism as a response to modern nominalism and skepticism. He has had essays published in such journals as the *American Catholic Philosophical Quarterly, International Philosophical Quarterly, Nova et Vetera*, and *Heythrop Journal*.

Gregory J. Kerr is Associate Professor of Philosophy at DeSales University in Center Valley, Pennsylvania. He received his B.A. and M.A. in philosophy from Boston College and his Ph.D. from Fordham University, where he did his dissertation on Maritain's Receptive Intuition and the Benefits of Art. He was a former editor of the *Maritain Notebook,* the official newsletter of the American Maritain Association. He has published articles on aesthetics, epistemology, science, ethics, and education in volumes in the AMA's series and elsewhere. Currently, he is finishing a volume that explores Maritain's surprising view on the very different and often conflicting ways humans know.

Matthew Minerd, Ph.L, is a professor of Philosophy and Moral Theology at the Byzantine Catholic Seminary of Ss. Cyril and Methodius in Pittsburgh.

Catherine Peters is Assistant Professor at Loyola Marymount University in Los Angeles, California. She earned her doctorate at the Center for Thomistic Studies at the University of St. Thomas in Houston, Texas. Peters specializes in medieval thought (in particular the work of Thomas Aquinas and Avicenna) and predominantly works on metaphysics and natural philosophy.

Scott J. Roniger is a doctoral candidate in Philosophy at The Catholic University of America. He holds graduate degrees in philosophy from the University of Chicago and the Pontifical University of the Holy Cross in Rome, and he has also published on Aristotle's *Metaphysics.*

CALL FOR PAPERS: Volume 5, 2020

We are accepting proposals for *Lex Naturalis* Volume 5, 2020. All topics related to natural law are welcome.

Abstracts (300–500 words) are due by January 15, 2020. Completed papers (25–30 pages) are due by August 15, 2020.

All submissions should be sent as an email attachment to Walter Raubicheck, Editor, at wraubicheck@pace.edu

Contributors

Address all submissions and correspondence to The Editor, LEX NATURALIS, Pace University, Department of Philosophy & Religious Studies, 1 Pace Plaza, New York, NY 10038. Please send two copies of the paper submitted. Include adequate margins, double space everything (text, notes, works cited, quotations). Use U.S. spelling and punctuation style (e.g. periods inside quotation marks; "double quotes" for opening and closing quotations). The University of Chicago Manual of Style, 17th Edition, is to be consulted regarding matters of style. Notes are to be numbered consecutively (in Arabic numerals) and placed at the bottom of the page.

Subscribers

Lex Naturalis is published annually by Pace University Press, 41 Park Row, Room 1510, New York, NY 10038. Subscription price: $40. Please send all subscription inquires to: PaceUP@pace.edu

www.ingramcontent.com/pod-product-compliance
Lightning Source LLC
Chambersburg PA
CBHW061830220326
41599CB00027B/5242

* 9 7 8 1 9 3 5 6 2 5 3 6 0 *